D1641804

Kristine Kimmi's book, *Created for the Extraordinary: You Were Made for Adventure, Not Fear,* is a must-read for anyone held back by fear but wanting to boldly step into the call God has for their life. Read this book or book her at your next event and learn from one of the most faith-driven and sincere women I know.

Niccie Kliegl
Author and Founder
of *Fulfill Your Legacy*

In her new book, Kristine invites readers on a journey to explore what it looks like when we discover who we are in Jesus and exchange a life lived in our power for a Spirit-led life fueled by God's power. It is truly in this moment when the real adventure begins.

Joan Turley
Author of *Sacred Work* and
Made to Make a Difference

A captivating and thought-provoking read! This book encouraged me to re-examine my faith journey and look for opportunities to live without fear!

J J Brotton
Instructor of Marketing
Kansas State University

Created for the Extraordinary

You Were Made for Adventure, Not Fear

Created for the Extraordinary

You Were Made for Adventure, Not Fear

Kristine Kimmi

Created for the Extraordinary
Copyright © 2022 by Kristine Kimmi, LLC
All rights reserved.
Printed in the United States of America

Published by Author Academy Elite
P.O. Box 43, Powell, OH 43065
www.AuthorAcademyElite.com

All rights reserved. No part of this publication may be reproduced, stored in a retrieval system, or transmitted in any form or by any means—for example, electronic, photocopy, recording—without the prior written permission of the publisher. The only exception is brief quotations in printed reviews.

Paperback ISBN: 978-1-64746-852-1
Hardcover ISBN: 978-1-64746-853-8
Ebook ISBN: 978-1-64746-854-5
Library of Congress Control Number: 2021912585

All Scripture quotations, unless otherwise indicated, are taken from the Holy Bible, New International Version®, NIV®. Copyright © 1973, 1978, 1984, 2011 by Biblica, Inc.™ Used by permission of Zondervan. All rights reserved worldwide. www.zondervan.com The "NIV" and "New International Version" are trademarks registered in the United States Patent and Trademark Office by Biblica, Inc. ™

[Notice of copyright for print and audio works quoting from the ESV]
Scripture quotations marked ESV are from the ESV® Bible (The Holy Bible, English Standard Version®), Copyright © 2001 by Crossway, a publishing ministry of Good News Publishers. Used by permission. All rights reserved.

[Notice of copyright for digital works quoting from the ESV]
Scripture quotations marked ESV are from the ESV® Bible (The Holy Bible, English Standard Version®), Copyright © 2001 by Crossway, a publishing ministry of Good News Publishers. Used by permission. All rights reserved. May not copy or download more than 500 consecutive verses of the ESV Bible or more than one half of any book of the ESV Bible.

Scripture quotations marked MSG are taken from THE MESSAGE, copyright © 1993, 2002, 2018 by Eugene H. Peterson. Used by permission of NavPress, represented by Tyndale House Publishers. All rights reserved.

Scripture quotations marked NKJV are taken from the New King James Version®. Copyright © 1982 by Thomas Nelson. Used by permission. All rights reserved.

Scripture quotations marked (NLT) are taken from the Holy Bible, New Living Translation, copyright ©1996, 2004, 2015 by Tyndale House Foundation. Used by permission of Tyndale House Publishers, Carol Stream, Illinois 60188. All rights reserved.

Any internet addresses (websites, blogs, etc.) printed in this book are provided as a resource. The author and publisher do not endorse them or vouch for their content or permanence.

The stories in this book have been recounted to the best of each source's recollection. To protect the privacy of certain individuals, some names have been changed.

DEDICATION

To Tony, for always believing in me and encouraging me to follow God's plans for my life. Thank you for your spoken words over me in the very beginning—the projected vision—I didn't have yet for myself. I love you more than you could ever imagine. You are truly God's gift to me.

To Alexis, Tarin and Jed, Taylor, Eve, and Elsie—I believe that God led me to write this book with each of you in mind. Never forget that with Him, anything is possible. I love you to the moon and back.

CONTENTS

Dedication ix

Acknowledgments xiii

Introduction xv

Part 1: Living in Fear

Chapter 1: What If? Why Not? 3

Chapter 2: Never Say Never 8

Chapter 3: The Spirit Connection 18

Chapter 4: When God Turns Your Plans Upside Down. . 22

Chapter 5: So Many Obstacles. 31

Part 2: Living in God's Power

Chapter 6: New Beginnings. 43

Chapter 7: Standing up under Pressure 47

Chapter 8: Sweet Dreams 53

Chapter 9: Out of My Comfort Zone 62

Chapter 10: Yes, No, Wait.........................70

Chapter 11: Meet Me in Las Vegas..................79

Part 3: Living the Adventure

Chapter 12: Living Each Day with Intention.........91

Chapter 13: Praying Bold Prayers 102

Chapter 14: Are You Ready? 119

Chapter 15: Adventure Involves Risk...............125

About the Author 131

Notes 133

ACKNOWLEDGMENTS

Karen and Doug, Mom (Joyce), Aunt Pat, Uncle Kal, J.J. and Dave, Robbin, Kristy, and Joan—Thank you for the many different ways you have provided kindness, support, encouragement, and feedback along the way.

Niccie Kliegl—Thank you for your friendship and mentorship as I have worked through the process of writing this book.

Alex Plagge and Felicity Fox—Thank you for using your editing gifts to help prepare this book for publication.

Family and friends who have covered me in prayer—Thank you for helping me to battle the spiritual warfare that I have often felt while writing the words on these pages.

Author photo courtesy of Brice Musgrove, Images by Brice
Cover art by Cindy McAlexander, Ocean Breeze Paintings (Etsy)

INTRODUCTION

Fear and anxiety: For some, it can be debilitating. For others, it may present as a subtle undercurrent, running right below the surface. We often define it as worry, which seems more acceptable.

I asked a friend in the mental health field about the concerns on people's minds today. She said self-image and fear of failure seem to be at the root of many anxiety-related issues regarding relationships, careers, finances, and family. Others have health and safety concerns or uneasiness about the state of politics in our world.

Maybe you find yourself thinking about some of these things. We all deal with fear and anxiety at some point in time. It's something that I have struggled with too. When I was young, I looked under the bed and in my closet before going to sleep every night.

In our household, we always watched the weekly movie or a drama series, most of which contained some pretty serious themes. One of those was a movie on the Bermuda (Devil's) Triangle. The other was a medical drama show, and one particular episode had a storyline involving a demon-possessed man. There is a common theme in both of these memories: Satan and demons, images still embedded in my mind.

Looking back, there were other moments that filled my mind with fear. I grew up on my grandparents' farm, a half-mile outside of our small town. It was a time when people felt relatively safe and often left their doors unlocked, especially during the day. But I remember waking up in the middle of the night to barking dogs and my dad listening at the back door because he said someone was trying to siphon gas out of a large gas tank. I think I understood from an early age that danger and evil exist. The things that we see, or experience, can have a huge impact on how we view the world.

You see, Satan knows the importance of what goes into our minds and how those things influence our thoughts. He knows the plans God has for our lives and will do anything to stop them.

Fear may be his greatest weapon against us.

My husband, Tony, was a wrestler in high school. He always said, "Wherever the head goes, the body will follow." This is also true when it comes to our minds. What we choose to focus on will dictate the direction we take. If Satan can direct our attention away from God, he already has us in a favorable position, and if he can fill our minds with fear, he knows it can immobilize us and make us ineffective for God.

The Bible tells us that "God has not given us a spirit of fear, but of power and of love and of a sound mind" (2 Timothy 1:7 NKJV). Ordinarily, fear seems like a negative thing, yet we are told to "fear God and keep his commandments" (Ecclesiastes 12:13 ESV). This is not the kind of fear that makes us afraid that God is waiting for us to make a mistake so He can *punish* us. Rather, healthy fear toward God is *reverence* toward Him. It helps us shun evil and cling to what is good, protects us, and reminds us of who He is and who we are as His children. Our God is awe-inspiring.

But Satan has a way of twisting things. When our fear is misplaced and everything and everyone becomes bigger in our minds than God, the enemy uses it to keep us from all God has planned. We can choose to live ordinary lives and struggle to do things in our power, or we can align ourselves with God and allow His power to work in and through us and live extraordinary lives.

INTRODUCTION

Life as a Christian is not boring. Do you believe that? If not, we need to talk. You may be following *religion*, but you don't know *God* because life with God is anything but boring.

I grew up in the church, read my Bible, prayed, and thought I knew God. But God, in His loving-kindness, began to show me that there is so much *more*, and it brings everything else to life.

He calls us to a life in the Spirit, full of adventure. God will often ask us to step outside of our comfort zones so we have to rely on His power and not our own. But I believe this is when we begin to see all the possibilities. He calls us to risk everything for Him because what He has done, and offers, is *that* good.

Years ago, God spoke Psalm 96:3 to me: "Declare his glory among the nations, his marvelous deeds among all peoples," and He continued to remind me of those words. I lived in a small town and didn't know anyone who was doing what I believed God was leading me to do, and I didn't truly understand the connection between surrender and seeing God's power at work. Still unclear about the way things work in God's economy, I hung onto my agenda—what I thought I needed to do—which was based on the world's standards.

God had to lead me through a process to change my thinking. He began to teach me that I had to be willing to risk it all for Him—to be okay with feeling uncomfortable—which goes against everything that seems natural. I had to learn how to let go and allow Him to be in control.

He has been showing me how to listen for His voice, trust Him, and run my race with boldness. My hope is that the message He has given me will help you to do the same. He has a good plan for my life and yours too. Perhaps you don't know Jesus personally. If that's the case, I hope you will go on this adventure with me. There's so much that God wants to show you. What do you have to lose?

PART 1

Living in Fear

Chapter One
WHAT IF? WHY NOT?

I climbed to the top of the high dive at summer camp in junior high and froze. Fear gripped me as I looked at the long board hanging over the water. After probably only a minute—but it felt like hours—I mustered up enough courage to jump and never went on the high dive again. Heights frightened me. Even the thought of flying in my dad's small airplane or in a helicopter while on vacation filled me with anxiety.

My sister, on the other hand, had less fear and a more adventurous personality. Our perceptions of things were vastly different. She married a man with an even more adventurous nature. These days, with a few more years under her belt and three children, she uses the words "What if?" more often, and my brother-in-law says, "Why not?"

I have always wondered what makes some people throw caution to the wind and take great leaps of faith while others struggle. My brother-in-law says it's because both types are necessary. If everyone had the "Why not?" mindset and acted impulsively instead of analyzing everything, no one would have ever lived long enough to settle the West.

But does it really have to be one or the other? What if you could somehow combine the two mindsets' highest qualities and live the best possible life? I have always wanted to be brave, but *my* power greatly lacks. Life is uncertain, and evil exists in the world. Everything seems bigger, stronger, and out of reach, so we can spend our lives holding back, settling for what we perceive as the surer, safer, and easier thing. But is that really living?

I want to make the most of every opportunity—to live full-on for God and all the plans He has for me.

How about you?

What if the safest and surest place to be is in the center of God's will, no matter what it looks like, and what if our perception of safety is in the center of the enemy's plans for our lives? What if they're flipped, our perception is skewed, and there's a different reality—one that would enable us to live the lives we've always wanted but never knew how to attain?

God loves you more than you could ever imagine. He knew you before you were even born and created you for a purpose, one designed specifically with you in mind.

> *For you created my inmost being; you knit me together in my mother's womb. Your eyes saw my unformed body; all the days ordained for me were written in your book before one of them came to be.*
>
> Psalm 139:13,16

> *For we are God's handiwork, created in Christ Jesus to do good works, which God prepared in advance for us to do.*
>
> Ephesians 2:10

> *See what great love the Father has lavished on us, that we should be called children of God!*
>
> 1 John 3:1

He also gave you free will—the ability to want more of Him or to walk away from Him.

I believe there is also a third choice, space where many believers find themselves. We may decide to trust God for our salvation through Jesus, so we can go to heaven when we die, but still refuse to trust Him completely with our lives while living here on earth.

Personality and life experience certainly influence a person's level of fearlessness, but what if there's something more at play here? You also have an enemy. Satan knows who you are. He hates God and all God has made, including you. The enemy's mission is to do everything within his power to see that you never fulfill God's plans for your life.

Be alert and of sober mind. Your enemy the devil prowls around like a roaring lion looking for someone to devour.
1 Peter 5:8

What if your whole journey is about God drawing you toward your purpose, energizing you for the work He has called you to do, and equipping you to deal with the enemy's interference along the way?

Your enemy is out to destroy you, and he will use any method necessary within the limitations God places upon him—whatever he knows will have an effect on you. Short of taking you completely out of the game, fear may be his greatest weapon against you.

For our struggle is not against flesh and blood, but against the rulers, against the authorities, against the powers of this dark world and against the spiritual forces of evil in the heavenly realms.
Ephesians 6:12

It was never God's intention for you to go through this life alone, and if you don't truly understand your identity as His child, it will be impossible for you to live as He has planned.

The moment we surrender it all to God is the point at which everything begins to change.

Everything.

When all we know and see are of this world, it can paralyze us and lead to an identity crisis. But when God reveals Himself and we begin to understand and see things that are not of this world, it empowers us to live His plan boldly. We begin to fear less, not because of our power, but because of His power that is at work within us through the Holy Spirit.

When you understand who you are in Jesus and refuse to allow fear to dominate your life, nothing can stop God's plans for you.

Nothing.

I believe it's time that we truly begin to understand who we were created to be so we can walk boldly in freedom, purpose, and power, and embrace the extraordinary life that God has designed for us.

We only get one shot at this life. How do you want to live yours?

Are you ready for a change—to go all-in and trust God with everything?

I promise it will be your greatest adventure and the best decision you have ever made. Hands down.

God loves you, and He has a wonderful plan for your life.

Do you struggle with fear and anxiety? In what ways?

Chapter Two
NEVER SAY NEVER

Do you trust God with everything? What if He asked you to change jobs or move to another city? What if His desire is for you to adopt rather than have biological children? How would you feel if you heard those dreaded words, "You have cancer?" Do you trust Him with your dreams, your family, your future? These are some of the questions my family and I have wrestled with over the years.

We want to control our lives and believe that we can do and be anything—we feel we largely define our destinies. The truth of the matter is that we do have choices and can choose to forge our own paths and reap the consequences, or we can choose to seek God and His will for our lives and follow the way He sets before us.

I was raised in the church, baptized, and accepted Jesus as my Lord and Savior at ten years old. During my teen years, I played the piano for worship services, participated in the youth group, and attended summer camp and Christian conferences. I knew who God was and prayed, read my Bible, and tried to follow the rules to the best of my ability.

But I wish I would have understood then what I know now. You can do all the *right* things and still not *really* know God or understand who you are in Jesus and the power made available to us by the Holy Spirit in the name of Jesus Christ.

In fact, I have a confession to make: Even now, I don't understand everything and probably won't until I get to heaven. However, one thing I know for sure is that since surrendering to God's plans for my life to the best of my ability, He has been teaching me what it looks like to live life in the Spirit. It takes an intentional desire for us to really know Him. But God is faithful, and if you ask Him to reveal Himself more fully to you, He will.

There's so much more than we can see and hear with our earthly eyes and ears, but we have to ask God to give us eyes to see and ears to hear so we can understand things the way He does. We have to allow the Holy Spirit to move in greater ways. When we surrender and ask God to take control of our lives and He begins to reveal Himself and His plans for us, it changes everything. You will never want to go back to the way things were before.

Your best life is found in Jesus, and although the journey is not always an easy one, it's full of adventure.

Surrender is the key that unlocks the door to everything God wants to do in your life, and the Holy Spirit is the source of power that helps you to accomplish His plans. You don't need to be fearful, but you do need to be Spirit-filled, and God is more than willing to help you if you will just ask.

Dealing with the Unexpected

I am not in control, yet I still struggle with this at times. Do you? When good things happen, we know how to react, but when the unexpected happens, we can perceive it negatively, which can fill our minds with fear. Over the years, I have learned that God is in control and that He always has a plan. Nothing is a surprise to Him. He knew about it before it happened, and He knew the outcome.

> *I make known the end from the beginning, from ancient times, what is still to come. I say, "My purpose will stand, and I will do all that I please."*
>
> Isaiah 46:10

So, if I believe God loves me and only wants the best for me, why do I still feel anxious and afraid when something unexpected drops into my life?

My husband, Tony, hadn't planned on losing his first job out of college—on his birthday. It was 1994, we had two young children at the time, and during the seven months before he began his new job, I became pregnant with baby number three. Life is full of the unexpected. But God is always faithful to fulfill His plans for our lives if we will give Him everything and simply trust Him.

Looking back, I believe with all my heart that God didn't want Tony at his former place of employment. God knew things that we didn't and protected our family and prepared us for something much better.

It had been nearly six months since Tony began his management trainee program with his new company, and we waited to find out where his first assignment would take us. I remember praying that it could be anywhere as long as it was in the eastern and not the western, less populated part of the state. I knew my wants and hoped that God would comply. But I soon learned to be careful about uttering those words—"I will never"—because God has a way of showing us who is in control of every situation, and I was learning that it wasn't me.

Just a few months after our youngest daughter was born, the transfer took us to Western Kansas, away from family and a built-in support system. I was a stay-at-home mom with a new baby, a two-year old, and a seven-year-old. The move was a big adjustment. In many ways, it was my time in the desert, but God had a master plan.

NEVER SAY NEVER

We began to attend a tiny church in town because it was a familiar denomination. During the first three years, we were very active and served in a number of ways. I even taught Sunday school classes and played music for worship.

However, as time went on, I began to feel spiritually empty and started listening to two well-known Christian speakers on the radio every morning because I needed the encouragement their messages provided.

We left the tiny church during our last year of living in the small town and attended another larger, more vibrant church. It was better in many ways, but we were already hoping for an opportunity to move back closer to home.

The *desert* is difficult in many ways, but one thing is certain: Things do grow there, and my trust in God and His power would be one of them.

So often, the desert seems to be a time of refining because it is during our greatest struggles when we turn to God and receive some of our greatest blessings. I was truly thirsty to grow in my faith and to know Him more, and God was faithful to meet me in my place of need.

As I walked through the doors of our small-town bookstore on a cold January day in 1999, I knew what I had gone there to buy and quickly scanned the titles. Unable to locate the book, I prayed, *Lord, show me the one you want me to read.*

One of the beautiful things about living a God-centered life is that very often, instead of giving us exactly what we *think* we want, He will give us what He knows we need.[1]

I browsed for a short time, waiting for something to jump out at me and picked up *Let Prayer Change Your Life* by Becky Tirabassi. As I read the back cover, the words "prayer warrior" caught my attention and brought to mind a recent conversation with my sister about how our maternal grandmother was also a prayer warrior.[2] I knew of my desire to be one as well. It clicked, and I purchased the book, along with its accompanying journal, *My Partner Prayer Notebook*, not realizing how much it would impact my life in the days to come.

Although I had always prayed, Tirabassi's book challenged me to have a more disciplined prayer life, setting aside as much as an hour each day to read my Bible, pray, and write down what I believed God was saying to me. Journaling my prayers and listening for God's voice became an important habit. I didn't realize it at the time, but God was setting the course for a life-changing experience in prayer, faith, and His power. Writing down the many details would provide me with a record of His faithfulness at every stage of the journey.

> *Only be careful, and watch yourselves closely so that you do not forget the things your eyes have seen or let them fade from your heart as long as you live. Teach them to your children and to their children after them.*
>
> Deuteronomy 4:9

Changes Ahead

We had lived in the small western Kansas town for about four years, and while it had been wonderful for Tony's career, it had also been a very challenging time in my life, producing an ever-increasing desire to move back to the eastern part of the state. Tony periodically reviewed the job announcements for open positions within his company and then shared them with me when he came home at the end of the day. But never before had a position opened up that seemed to be the right one.

Three days after purchasing the book on prayer, a newly created position posted: Legislative Analyst. I had been watching C-Span's legislative hearings and was very intrigued. In the past, Tony had assured me that he didn't have any interest in politics or in putting himself or his family under the media's microscope. However, Legislative Analyst sounded interesting, so he went back to work after lunch and called his boss to ask about the salary. The listed amount wasn't enough to meet our family's needs, so we asked God to give us a sign if He wanted Tony to apply for the position because we didn't see how we could do it otherwise.

The next morning, Tony's boss called to let him know that he had been to a business meeting the night before and had heard about this newly created position's salary. It wasn't necessarily going to be as low as he had thought. Though the salary amount was still up in the air, we knew this was our prayed-for sign.

After talking to Tony on the phone, I opened *Joseph* (by Charles Swindoll), the book we were studying in our Sunday school class. A bookmark had been shoved into the middle of the book to a place we had not yet read, and on the page was this challenge:

> *Stay open to a new idea for at least five minutes.* Don't try it for an entire day, because you'll almost panic. Just take on your day five minutes at a time. When something new, something unexpected, confronts you, don't respond with an immediate "Nope! Never!" Wait five minutes. Hold off. Tolerate the possibility for five minutes. You could be surprised at the benefit of remaining open those three hundred seconds.[3]

I knew God had orchestrated this as an encouragement for us. Then, the following words came to mind: "Now to him who is able to do immeasurably more than all we ask or imagine, according to his power that is at work within us" (Ephesians 3:20).

The next day, Tony's boss signed the transfer sheet, and we waited.

As I prayed about these things, I started to notice that specific biblical passages (book, chapter, and verse) would flash into my mind. I didn't know some of the verses off the top of my head, but when I read them, they spoke perfectly to the situation at hand:

> *However, as it is written: "What no eye has seen, what no ear has heard, and what no human mind has conceived"— the things God has prepared for those who love him.*
>
> 1 Corinthians 2:9

> *Be still before the LORD and wait patiently for him.*
>
> Psalm 37:7

I didn't want to appear foolish when I shared these things. We were discussing plans to move, even though Tony had not yet been invited for an interview. However, I knew God was speaking to us. All of these things were not merely coincidences, and I didn't want to disappoint God by showing a lack of faith when I believed something good was going to happen.

During this time, the man in charge of preparing for the interviews told Tony that he had put in a recommendation for him. Around fifty resumes came through—some from attorneys and lobbyists. My initial reaction was concern, but those feelings quickly gave way to hope and inspiration. Under the challenging circumstances, I knew that if Tony got the job, it would be because God wanted him there. He couldn't take the credit. All the glory would be given to God "who is able to do immeasurably more than all we ask or imagine" (Ephesians 3:20).

Tony went through two rounds of interviews as they continued to narrow down the list of candidates, and God continued to place verses in my mind to sustain us through His word while we waited: "The LORD will indeed give what is good, and our land will yield its harvest. Righteousness goes before him and prepares the way for his steps" (Psalm 85:12–13).

After nearly seven weeks of waiting, Tony called to say they had offered him the job.

We were moving!

During that almost two-month period when I shared what I believed God was doing, my words were often met with unbelief. It was as if some of those closest to us believed we would face disappointment. Others who hoped that we would not move seemed encouraged because I was unable to provide them with new information along the way.

At the time, it frustrated me, but I had to realize that it was okay if they didn't understand because it wasn't their journey. It was ours. God was speaking to *us* about our circumstances, not them.

And no one and nothing can interfere with God's plans.[4]

Everything seemed connected, from reading *Joseph* in Sunday school, to buying, reading, and applying the principles from *Let Prayer Change Your Life,* to the announcement of the newly created position. It was all a perfectly designed and executed plan by God to not only move us to another part of the state (our desire) but to grow our prayer lives and trust in Him.

I had always prayed but had never experienced the wonders of God in the same way until I dedicated myself to praying every day and writing down the message I believed God was conveying. He was opening up another world to me, and it changed the way I viewed prayer and my relationship with Him from that day forward.

God became real to me in a way I had not understood before. I no longer saw Him as distant. Instead, I saw Him as my heavenly Father who loved me enough to make Himself known to me in a much more tangible way.

What about you? How do you view God? Do you see Him as someone who simply watches and judges everything on this earth from afar, or do you see Him as someone who loves you and wants to be intimately involved in your life?

It was also during this time when God began to plant a seed in my heart concerning writing and speaking about everything that He was showing me. But at the time, I believed I needed to finish my college degree. I didn't feel equipped to write and speak publicly about all the wonderful things He was doing. There was still so much to learn about trusting God, the One who gives each of us our unique gifts and prepares us to use them for His glory.[5] His view of success is often different from the world's, and God's power brings all new things to life.

Surrender is the key that unlocks the door to everything God wants to do in your life.

How do you view God? Do you see Him as someone who watches and judges everything from afar, or do you see Him as someone who wants to be intimately involved in your life?

Do you look forward to spending time with God, or do you view it as just another task on your list of things to do? Describe your personal time with God. What do you enjoy most?

What thing(s) do you need to give God control of in your life?

Chapter Three
THE SPIRIT CONNECTION

I used to think the Holy Spirit is simply our conscience that lets us know when we do something wrong. While that's part of His job (John 16:8), He is so much more. Did you know that God communicates with us through His Spirit? How cool is that?

As Jesus neared the end of His time on earth and prepared to go to the cross for you and me, He told His disciples about the Holy Spirit who would come to them after His ascension to heaven. Jesus told them, "If you love me, keep my commands. And I will ask the Father, and he will give you another advocate to help you and be with you forever—" (John 14:15–16). The Spirit would be God's power living inside of them (Acts 1:5,8), and He would do the following things for them:

- "Teach [them] all things" (John 14:26).
- "Remind [them] of everything [Jesus had] said to [them]" (John 14:26).
- "Guide [them] into all the truth" (John 16:13).
- "Tell [them] what is yet to come" (John 16:13).

Can you imagine what it must have been like for the disciples? They spent so much time with Jesus, while He taught them and invested in their lives. However, Jesus said that very soon He would leave but that they would not be alone because He would send the Holy Spirit. Jesus knew what was to come and tried to prepare them (John 16).

We cannot do what God has called us to do without the power of the Holy Spirit. Our power alone isn't strong enough to battle Satan and all his schemes, but when we surrender our lives to the lordship of Jesus Christ, the Holy Spirit (God's power) comes to live inside of us. When you feel scared, the Holy Spirit enables you to be bold for Christ (Acts 4:29–31). He "gives life" (John 6:63) and brings peace, hope, and joy (Romans 15:13, 14:17). Friend, He is your power source.

In fact, Jesus said, "Very truly I tell you, whoever believes in me will do the works I have been doing, and they will do even greater things than these, because I am going to the Father. And I will do whatever you ask in my name, so that the Father may be glorified in the Son. You may ask me for anything in my name, and I will do it" (John 14:12–14).

We have work to do and a helper who will enable us to do it.

After Jesus died on the cross, was buried, and God raised Him to life again (Matthew 27–28), He appeared to His disciples before ascending into heaven and left them with a call to action: "All authority in heaven and on earth has been given to me. Therefore go and make disciples of all nations, baptizing them in the name of the Father and of the Son and of the Holy Spirit, and teaching them to obey everything I have commanded you. And surely I am with you always, to the very end of the age" (Matthew 28:18–20).

Did you catch that? Jesus said He would *always* be with them.

What would this world look like if every believer understood the power living inside of us? What would *we* look like? When we understand how big God is and how much He loves us, we won't allow fear to stand in the way of what He calls us to.

The Holy Spirit is your source of power.

Are you aware of the Holy Spirit working in your life?
In what way(s) do you feel or sense His presence?

Chapter Four
WHEN GOD TURNS YOUR PLANS UPSIDE DOWN

It was 2002, and we had been in Manhattan, Kansas for nearly three years. During that time, God was teaching me to be content while I waited to accomplish my goals. I focused on my roles as wife and mom, took care of everything at home, volunteered to help with the school carnival, and taught Sunday school classes for junior high students at our church.

Family has always been my heart, and while I was thankful for the opportunity to be a stay-at-home mom, I knew God had created more for me to do. Because I was fairly certain those plans included writing, I asked Him to prepare me to write, to provide a publisher, and to give me a future job with the flexibility to set my hours and travel with Tony and his career when the kids were older.

With our youngest daughter, Taylor, in school all day, I enrolled in two university classes for the spring semester: Introduction to Literature Studies and Public Speaking. As a thirty-two-year-old, I was quite a bit older than most of the other students in my classes, but I had waited so long for this opportunity and loved the work (conducting research, writing, and speaking). It felt right, and I wondered what God had planned for my future when Tony came home one evening with some news.

"I want to take you out to dinner. I have something to tell you," Tony said. The urgency in his voice and my natural curiosity told me it was something I could not wait to hear, so I said, "Tell me now."

He answered, "How would you feel about moving to Iowa?" I didn't know much about Iowa except that it was a Midwestern state like Kansas, so I said, "I don't want to move to Iowa. The only thing in Iowa is corn."

Over dinner, I listened as Tony talked about his company's possible merger with another company, which meant his department would relocate to Iowa if everything went through.

Suddenly, my plans were changing. I thought we would probably live in Manhattan forever. I planned on finishing my degree, and our three daughters had lives and friends that were important to them. Why would God choose to move us now?

Tony was advised to research the Des Moines area, including living expenses and home prices, and come up with a salary that would meet our needs. I spent the next week researching the prices of homes, setting an ideal budget, and coming up with an annual salary to meet those needs. We did not discuss numbers with anyone. That way, if the offer matched, we could look at it as another sign that God was working on our behalf.

As I looked through an information packet about the Des Moines area, it was clear that the city had much to offer our family, which led to a growing sense of excitement for the many new opportunities. I also knew that if God wanted me to finish my education, He would provide a way.

The possible merger announcement was still months away, and we had to keep it quiet, which meant we had to live as if nothing would change. During this time, we relied on God to give us peace to know that He was in control of everything so we wouldn't worry.

After the announcement in July, we were finally able to tell our children. It was especially difficult for our oldest daughter, who would be a freshman in high school. Waiting filled the next five months—merger approval, decision making, and for Tony to learn his future position.

Finally, the day arrived when he was to have his meeting with human resources. His boss had told him to expect an offer for a director's position. However, at the meeting, he received news that an employee from another state had chosen not to move his family to Iowa. Therefore, Tony received the position of Product Development Vice President—a whole step above his originally projected position and an annual salary within $3,000 of what I had initially determined to be ideal. I knew that only God could have made it happen so perfectly.

In addition, the company offered the option of a buyout for our house in Manhattan so we wouldn't have to wait for it to sell—another huge blessing. Our family would be able to relocate together, making it an easier transition for all of us.

Over Christmas vacation, we traveled to Iowa to look at houses with a realtor. One property was our favorite because it had everything we wanted, including a large garage, a plus for Tony because it would provide space for woodworking. However, we could not commit to buying anything until we received the appraisals of our current house.

After only a few days, we returned to Manhattan. I continued to pray that God would provide the best home for our family and that He would let us know if this particular one was right for us.

Less than one week later, our realtor called and said that the seller was pressuring the relocation company to sell the house and that they wanted to work with us. She added that it was pretty much unheard of and rarely happened.

God had provided a way for us to have our most desired house. The following week, we received a call from the representative of the relocation company handling the buyout. She said that the appraisals had been completed but that she felt shocked because what usually took several weeks to accomplish was done in just a few days.

I told her we had been praying about it, and she said, "Well, it worked." The appraisals for our house in Manhattan were even higher than we had expected. God had provided more than enough money from the buyout, allowing us to purchase the home He had selected for us.

When you trust God and surrender to His plans for your life, He can do the seemingly impossible and accelerate the natural order of things.

In February, the moving company came and packed up our belongings. As we drove to West Des Moines the next day, I knew God was working on our behalf. But we were still moving away from a place we loved, which was difficult.

We pulled into town as darkness fell, and I prayed that God would show us someone we knew, something familiar. We had not eaten dinner, so we pulled up to a Perkins restaurant and went inside. As we waited to be seated, another couple from Manhattan—also relocating to Iowa—walked in behind us. There was no way to know we would all choose the same restaurant and arrive simultaneously. However, God knew my desire and made it happen.

He continued to prove His involvement in every detail of our move. We live in a big world, but it is comparatively small where our God is concerned.

We settled into our new home and the following week drove to a grocery store in West Des Moines to shop for food and supplies. The young man bagging groceries asked if we wanted "drive up." I said, "I don't know what that is. We just moved here." He asked where we came from and when I said, "Manhattan, Kansas," he told me that his extended family owned a small restaurant near Manhattan and that he and his immediate family were getting ready to move there in a couple of weeks.

Right then, I felt that home was not so far away. What were the odds that I would meet and speak with this young man who *just happened* to be moving to the town from where we had just moved?

God knows where you are and what you need, and He has the power to get you where you need to be and to connect you with the right people.[1]

Once again, I was completely humbled by my heavenly Father's power and kindness. He knew I missed Manhattan, and in this small way, He had brought it to me and reminded me that He was with me each step of the way and in control of everything and everyone who would cross my path.

I am forever amazed by what God can do. There is no such thing as *luck* to a Christian. God is always working in our lives, and nothing is out of His control. Sometimes, He asks us to make small changes. Other times, He asks us to make big changes, and we may not understand the reason behind His request. During these times, we must choose to walk in faith. If we believe that He always goes before us and that everything He does is for our good, how can we not follow?

I Am Doing Something New

With just three months left in the school year, we enrolled our three daughters in the public schools where we lived. Taylor (second grade) and Tarin (fourth grade) adjusted well. But the transition didn't go quite so smoothly for Alexis, who was finishing up her freshman year of high school.

We have been told that moving is one of the most stressful things anyone can experience. But as adults, we typically have some say in our circumstances. Children don't usually have the same level of control, and for a teenager, it can be challenging. Alexis had to leave behind everyone and everything familiar and start over. We shed many tears over those three months.

It hurt me to see her so sad inside.

We tried to do everything we knew to do as parents.

One of her teachers, who was also a track coach and involved with the school's Fellowship of Christian Athletes, encouraged her to join the track team. We were so thankful for his efforts, but she couldn't bring herself to accept the invitation. With concern for her well-being, I prayed for God to intervene and meet our daughter's needs in whatever way He determined would be best.

One day, I heard an advertisement on the radio for an open house at a private Christian academy located nearby. I wondered if this could be our answer.

So, I prayed and asked God to open her heart to the idea if it was His will for her.

When she arrived home from school, I asked if she would be interested in attending the open house. Without skipping a beat, she said, "Yes," and her visit to the school was everything she had hoped for *and more*. It had not been easy, but God was working out the details in our children's lives, and we were so grateful for all we saw Him doing.

In my quiet time, God spoke the following words to me:

I took you from the ends of the earth, from its farthest corners I called you. I said, "You are my servant"; I have chosen you and have not rejected you.

Isaiah 41:9

Forget the former things; do not dwell on the past. See, I am doing a new thing! Now it springs up; do you not perceive it? I am making a way in the wilderness and streams in the wasteland.

Isaiah 43:18–19

Declare his glory among the nations, his marvelous deeds among all peoples.

Psalm 96:3

I called you . . . I am doing a new thing . . . I am making a way . . . Declare my glory . . . my marvelous deeds.

With our daughters in school during the day, I joined a social group for women who were new to the area. I loved the opportunities that Des Moines offered. We had so much to be thankful for, and God had proven that He would provide for *all* our needs. However, one thing still remained on my mind: the desire to finish my education. And although the social group was wonderful, I couldn't shake the feeling that I wanted more.

God was whispering, *I am doing something new*, but I was still looking at what I had left behind because I thought I knew how things needed to unfold.

Some of you may be going through changes in your life that leave you feeling uncertain about your future. Perhaps you have a dream that God has placed in your heart, and you wonder how you are ever going to achieve it with so many responsibilities at home or a career that consumes all your time and energy. Maybe you have just been informed that changes are coming with your job and there is a possibility that your position may be eliminated or that a transfer is imminent. Our first reaction to these things is often to worry about what we don't know instead of saying, "Lord, I know nothing is out of your control. Help me to keep my eyes focused on you and to see your hand at work in this situation."

During the good and bad days, trust Him. When you can see what tomorrow will bring, trust Him. When you don't know how you will deal with the next hour, trust Him. Life is not always easy, but we serve a good God who loves us infinitely and promises to always be with us and make things happen for our benefit and His glory.

> *And we know that in all things God works for the good of those who love him, who have been called according to his purpose.*
>
> Romans 8:28

Paul doesn't say that everything in and of itself is good, only that God is in control, there is a reason for whatever He allows into our lives, and the result will be in accordance with His plans for us.

> *"For I know the plans I have for you," declares the LORD, "plans to prosper you and not to harm you, plans to give you hope and a future."*
>
> Jeremiah 29:11

The path to the promise is not always free of trials. In fact, life is seldom free of trials. As much as we dislike them, it's often during the difficult times when we cling to God more. Our faith increases as He lifts us above the waves and moves mountains on our behalf.[2]

I am in awe of all that is God. He is always creating, and His work is always good. If we can trust Him to do the same work in our lives, no matter how things appear at the time, the end result will amaze us. "For nothing [is] impossible with God" (Luke 1:37 ESV).

God can do the seemingly impossible and accelerate the natural order of things.

Has God ever turned your plans upside down? Describe the situation. How did it make you feel? How were you able to see His hand at work?

Chapter Five
SO MANY OBSTACLES

In the fall of 2004, a year and a half after moving our family to Iowa, Alexis began her second year at the private Christian academy. She looked forward to another season on the basketball team and her first job. Taylor joined a soccer team, and Tarin eagerly anticipated softball season. For the most part, things were going well, but we still needed to find a church that the whole family could agree upon.

We divided our two and a half years between a large church and a much smaller church plant that was still meeting in a local school. Both churches were wonderful, but Alexis struggled because no one from her school attended either one. What made it even more difficult was that she had loved our church in Manhattan.

Tarin and Taylor also found it challenging to feel at home in either church. As I prayed to God, I reminded Him that He had moved us there, and I knew that if we were within His will, He already had a plan in place for us. He wanted our children to grow in their faith and knowledge of Him as much as we did.

What do we do, Lord? I prayed. *You moved us here. We feel like we are within your will for our lives. Now what?*

That same month, the Holy Spirit led me to the following verse in Ezekiel, and as I read it, I recorded it in my prayer journal: "'But you, mountains of Israel, will produce branches and fruit for my people Israel, for they will soon come home.'"[1]

The words "they will soon come home" stood out in my mind, and I wondered if God, in His grace and mercy, was letting me know He would eventually move us back to Manhattan.

One month later, the head of another department approached Tony and asked if he had ever thought about moving back to Manhattan. It seemed that an opportunity might present itself in the future. Neither of us knew what to think about the proposition. We were intrigued at the thought of moving back but wondered if this was truly God's will for our lives.

Less than six months later, company reorganization created a new position—in Manhattan. We felt torn between accepting the job and staying in Iowa to allow Alexis to finish her senior year. We just couldn't bring ourselves to move her again at that point in time, so Tony turned down the offer. It felt like we were closing the door on our final opportunity to move back home. I loved Des Moines but missed so many things of home, and some of those things—our church and the university—were pulling me back.

If you have moved in your life, you understand the roller coaster ride of emotions. To never look back and feel sad means that you felt no connection to where you were living. To be torn between two places means that you have fond memories and ties to both—a true blessing—but it also makes it a difficult choice to leave one place for the other. We found ourselves longing for our old home but sad to leave our new home behind. I often wished I could combine the things I loved from both into one place.

Two months later, Tony received the offer again. Our hope to hold out for another year was dashed, and we were forced to make a decision one way or the other. When I mentioned our dilemma to Alexis, she replied, "What if I would want to move back to Manhattan?"

Her question stopped me in my tracks. We talked it over, and I told her that if she said yes today, she would most likely change her mind tomorrow. She said that she understood and didn't know why her feelings had changed but that she had been praying about it.

I knew we had witnessed a miracle. God understood our inability to make a decision that would bring pain to our daughter and, in His sovereignty, took it out of our hands. Only He could have changed her mind, confirming our belief that this move—no matter how it looked from the outside—was part of His plan.

Her words set everything into motion. I called Tony at work to tell him. In return, he called his soon-to-be boss and accepted the position but asked for time to notify everyone involved.

Just as I suspected and cautioned her about, the next morning, Alexis changed her mind again. She was still wrestling with the decision like the rest of us. But by then, it was too late.

Nothing and no one can prevent God from accomplishing His objectives in our lives. What He declares *will* happen, even when the odds are stacked against it.

If you know God is asking you to do something but all you can see are the obstacles in front of you, trust Him to work out all of the details, large and small. Never say never because "nothing [is]impossible with [our] God."[2]

God always has a plan, and if we trust Him even when things don't make sense from a human perspective, we stand to gain everything in return.

Mountains of Unbelief

We moved back to Manhattan in the summer of 2005. The following January, I returned to the university to finish my undergraduate degree. Some semesters, I only took classes part-time because I was trying to balance school and family. But in the spring of 2010, I finally graduated with a Bachelor of Arts in English and a minor in French.

I think most people finish the last exam of their college career and are thankful to be done, but I loved school. As I pulled out of the parking garage that day, I knew I would miss it. However, I was also ready for a *normal* life again—one where I could focus on my family without having to worry about completing homework and studying for tests.

Armed with my degree and a little more confidence, I was anxious to see what God had in mind for me. I read about a contest hosted by Guideposts Magazine. Winners had the opportunity to join other aspiring writers at the Guideposts Writers Workshop in New York for training and the possibility of having their story published. I decided to take a leap of faith and submitted my story but didn't win. Though disappointed, I knew there would be other opportunities. Some way. Somehow.

A few months later, I applied for a copywriter position with a local company and received an interview but was not offered the position. Soon after, my former undergraduate adviser from the university asked me to copyedit her project. I kept track of my hours, and she paid me accordingly.

I was excited to use my skills, and it strengthened my desire to pursue writing as a career, although I didn't know how I would accomplish my goal with the obstacles I saw in front of me. My lack of connections and belief that I needed to live in a big city like Chicago or New York, near publishing companies, seemed too large to overcome.

Instead of believing that God could do anything, the practical side of me won out once again, and I decided to return to school as a full-time graduate student. Not only was I accepted, but I also received a graduate teaching assistantship, which meant that I would teach Expository Writing in exchange for a tuition waiver and small stipend. It was what I wanted, and I was excited.

However, even though I loved taking classes and working with students, it left little time for anything else, including family. From 6:00 a.m. until 10:00 p.m. during the week, my days were almost entirely focused on school-related things. Weekends were busy, too, and I was only sleeping about five hours each night because of the stress.

I knew that if I had any hope of getting a job as an instructor after graduation, I would need to complete the two-year assistantship program. But I was exhausted at the end of the semester. Although I knew that some things would get easier with time, the reality was that I had to decide if it was worth it to my family and me.

I experienced some relief when I decided to give up teaching, but part of me felt like a failure.

In the days that led up to the spring semester, I spent more time with God. We talked about my priorities and dreams, and as I prayed, I asked Him, "How can I use my talents and gifts for you in light of these things?"

Immediately, Psalm 45 flashed into my mind, and as I read, the following words from verse one spoke to me: "My tongue is the pen of a skillful writer." I still had questions about how all of this would be possible and how I would be able to earn a living for my family, but I wanted so badly to be obedient and determined that the best thing would be to leave graduate school and focus on writing.

I was relieved to have my new-found freedom, but what I didn't realize at the time is that true freedom comes with full surrender to God. Only then do we gain clarity, and what I needed more than anything was Godly wisdom.

> *If you need wisdom, ask our generous God, and he will give it to you . . . But when you ask him, be sure that your faith is in God alone. Do not waver, for a person with divided loyalty is*

as unsettled as a wave of the sea that is blown and tossed by the wind. Such people should not expect to receive anything from the Lord. Their loyalty is divided between God and the world, and they are unstable in everything they do.

James 1:5–8 NLT

I was a little like the wave James talks about, wavering between what I knew the world was telling me to focus on and what I thought God wanted me to do. In my heart, I believed God wanted me to write about Christian living, but I didn't see how I could do that and get to where I thought I needed to be.

In my mind, there were too many obstacles.

And I still didn't get it.

One day in my office, as I thought about all of these things, I said, *Lord, if I write about matters of faith, I don't see how I'm ever going to be able to earn a living. What if only one or two people read what I write?* And in my spirit, I heard Him say, *What if only one or two people read what you write, but what if those are the people I want to read it?*

Now, let me be clear: God never said, "Only one or two people are ever going to read the words you write." However, I believe God was trying to help me understand what was at stake. What He was asking me to do wasn't about me. It was about Him and my willingness to trust Him, but I still hadn't surrendered enough to say, *Okay, Father. You're the boss. Let's do it.*

We can come up with all kinds of excuses for not obeying God. Obstacles exist, but if we believe our God is all-powerful, we will not let difficulties stop us from doing whatever we can do.

Maybe the only thing you believe you can do at the moment is pray. If you do what you can do, God will do what you cannot do.

SO MANY OBSTACLES

I didn't comprehend it at the time, but unbelief was my greatest obstacle.

When everything before us appears much bigger than God, we are experiencing a crisis of unbelief. I thought my circumstances needed to change before I could step into my calling, but I was the one who needed to change.

Maybe you find yourself there right now.

Friend, if God is preparing something for you, He will provide everything you need to accomplish those tasks.

Everything.

Maybe you don't have the money, but God can provide from the most unusual sources. Mentors? Opportunities? Yep. He has access to all of it.

> *And my God will meet all your needs according to the riches of his glory in Christ Jesus.*
> Philippians 4:19

God owns everything. He is rich beyond our ability to measure.

> *For every animal of the forest is mine, and the cattle on a thousand hills. I know every bird in the mountains, and the insects in the fields are mine. If I were hungry I would not tell you, for the world is mine, and all that is in it.*
> Psalm 50:10–12

It really boils down to how much we trust Him.

When we are serious about wanting to do God's will and believe anything is possible, God makes His presence and power known. Faith releases God's blessing.

If God asks you to do something, He is also going to take care of the details. It is not up to you to figure everything out. All you have to do is to remain in faith and do the next thing. He will get you there.

CREATED FOR THE EXTRAORDINARY

In October of 2012, I published my first blog post on my WordPress website, *Energized by Design*. It was titled "Seasons of Change" and focused on trusting God, taking risks, and having adventures.

One month later, I began to substitute teach for our local school district because teaching was in my blood. My mother, sister, and grandmother had all been teachers in the public school system, and I had taught Sunday school classes for years in different churches.

Even though teaching came naturally to me and I loved working with students, my degree was in English (subject matter), not education. I didn't have a teaching certificate but wanted to feel like a *real* teacher, so I had two choices: return to school for more than two years to obtain a teaching certificate or earn an MA in English, which would allow me to teach at the university level.

I loved the freedom that teaching at the university offered, so after one and a half years of substitute teaching, I decided to return to graduate school. Although I knew it would be challenging to juggle full-time school and a graduate teaching assistantship, I thought that a better understanding and the right attitude would allow for a different experience.

With great anticipation, I prayed about it, contacted the right people, and God opened the doors for me to return. By that time it was mid-June, and there were no more graduate teaching assistantships available. But to my surprise, one week before orientation, I received an email about teaching Expository Writing again. One of the students would not attend, after all, so there was an opening.

I was excited and accepted the offer. It was easier in some ways than it had been the first time around. However, I still didn't have the desired amount of time for my family, and I realized that if I were to work as an instructor following graduation, my busy schedule would not lighten. One professor told me that it gets even busier, so I decided to focus on finishing my MA in English with a concentration in Composition and Rhetoric but knew that God was calling me back to writing and speaking for Him. By then, I was ready to surrender and follow His call.

I will be forever grateful for the opportunity to go to graduate school and for those who poured into me during those years. It's an experience that I will never forget. For the longest time, I thought maybe graduate school was a wrong turn I had made on the road of life as I tried to navigate around obeying God's plans for me.

Now I believe God allowed me to do those other things (teaching and graduate school) because they were good training for my future, and He knew I would come around to His way of thinking eventually. Academia may not have been a permanent placement, but God could use those experiences to equip me for what was ahead.

God is so good, isn't He? His love and patience are never-ending.

Alexis also believes moving back to Manhattan was God's plan for her life. It enabled her to attend Manhattan Christian College, where she earned an associate degree and served as goalie for the soccer team. She also graduated from Kansas State University with a degree in Family Studies and Human Services and Park University with a Master of Public Administration degree. Her desire has always been to help make people's lives better.

We all have gifts and talents and dreams that are so clearly written into our DNA. They are pieces of who we are—things we cannot shake—that bring us great joy and contentment. We need to pay attention to these details because they are with us for a reason. God is our creator and our "builder" (Hebrews 3:4–6), and we are part of His plan. We only need to understand who He created us to be and what He created us to do. Then, we must trust that He will help us to complete the work.

If you trust Him, God can remove the obstacles in your way.

Have you ever experienced a crisis of unbelief in your life? What obstacles did you see in front of you that made it difficult to believe God was in control and would do the things He promised to do?

PART 2

Living in God's Power

Chapter Six
NEW BEGINNINGS

The summer of 2016 was a turning point in my life. I had finished graduate school and felt God leading me to let go of everything and focus on Him. I needed a reset—a time to rest and allow the Holy Spirit to renew my mind. Pulling away from all that the world was telling me I should be doing felt strange. Resting can feel lazy to us. We may sense that we should be doing something.

Anything.

Yet drawing closer to God and listening intently to His voice often requires us to slow down, find a quiet place, and allow Him to redirect our thoughts.

Isaiah 30:15 says, "In repentance and rest is your salvation, in quietness and trust is your strength . . ."

It was also a time of new beginnings for our youngest daughter, who had graduated from nursing school with her Associate of Nursing degree (RN). Anxiety grew as her friends accepted job offers, but she still wondered what God had prepared for her.

When Taylor began nursing school, her desire to travel and explore new things led her to research possible cities that she could move to upon graduation. She was drawn to Nashville and two years later had the opportunity to visit for the day on our way home from a conference.

That next spring as she prepared to graduate from nursing school, Taylor felt uncertain about where God wanted her. Looking for direction, she turned to Facebook and posted about her pursuit of a job in Nashville. One of her classmates from Tennessee told her to look in the Murfreesboro area.

As she searched job listings, she found a hospital residency program in Murfreesboro. To her surprise, the hospital's two campuses in Nashville (Midtown and West) offered the same program, so she applied for acceptance to the October cohort. Less than two weeks later, she received an email with an invitation to interview for the July cohort. It was a whirlwind as she opened the email on a Thursday, and we drove to Nashville the following Monday for her Tuesday interview.

She received an invitation to join the residency programs at Midtown and West, and she chose Midtown. At her request, Tony and I drove around and looked at housing options. We even stopped by a church that Taylor had found online and asked the receptionist if she could give us some advice. Using information that she provided, we narrowed our search.

After we picked up Taylor and ate lunch, we went back to the hotel and made an appointment to see one of the buildings close to the hospital and another one for the next day. We quickly learned that a safe neighborhood close to her work was more money than she could afford. Anything less looked questionable. I prayed, "Lord, please give her a cherry of a place to live."

Our appointment later that afternoon was in a nice, clean, secure building with management on site every day. We toured a couple of apartments and loved everything we saw, except for the price. When we went back downstairs to talk with the management team, we learned that if she signed on immediately, they would drop the monthly price by over $300 and include garage parking, which would have been $50 extra each month. The $350 savings allowed her to grab the apartment.

As we drove away, my gratitude was at an all-time high, and I couldn't help but tear up as I said, "Thank you, God." I was so grateful that He had provided a wonderful place for her to live. As parents, we felt an enormous weight lift and knew she would be alright moving alone to the big city because God would be with her every step of the way.

I also knew that several Christian authors lived in the Nashville area, and Thomas Nelson Publishing Company's (publisher for Christian books and Bibles) headquarters was also in the city. This knowledge alone brought hope that God would connect me with someone who could help me with the work He was calling me to do. I had seen how He had changed everything in an instant for Taylor, and I knew He could do the same for me.

If you struggle to hear God's voice, spend more time in His presence. Open His word and ask Him to speak to you. He is in control and has the power to change everything in an instant, but we must trust Him and His timing.

How good are you at slowing down and taking time to rest in God? What is something that you need to trust Him for today? What step can you take, knowing that God will meet you there and provide for your every need?

Chapter Seven
STANDING UP UNDER PRESSURE

That September, I read Jennie Allen's book *Anything*, the story of her journey to follow God's plans for her life, including the founding of IF: Gathering.[1] Soon after, I applied and learned that I would have the opportunity to be part of the book launch for her new book *Nothing to Prove*, set to release in January 2017.[2] Her books were like water to my thirsty soul, ministering to me as I continued to release control of my life to God. It was also an opportunity to get a closer look at the book launching process.

During this time, God also spoke to me about starting to blog again, something I had begun in 2012 but stopped after only one post because I didn't really think anyone would read what I wrote. I struggled with following what I believed God was asking me to do and pursuing what I thought would be a more practical and financially lucrative path. The battle inside my head between God's thoughts and Satan's counterattack made me second-guess everything I believed.

My husband and my children supported me, and their encouraging words were like life-giving honey. I also knew that others didn't understand and wondered why this woman who had finished her master's degree didn't have a *real* job. My daughter has told me that I need to care less about what people think. To some degree, she is right, and God has been helping me with this issue.

There is always risk when sharing God's plans for our lives with others because of rejection or pushback, which often comes in the form of disinterest or lack of encouragement. But sometimes, people will try to push you toward something other than what you know God is asking you to do.

At times, it's possible to put distance between yourself and these people. But what can you do when creating space is nearly impossible?

Because I have been in this situation, I know the pain it can cause. Our first conversation took place at the beginning of the fall semester after I graduated. As Tony and I arrived at Marshall and Maggie's house to pick them up for dinner, we went inside for a few minutes. While Marshall showed Tony something in the garage, Maggie walked into the living room. We were the only ones there, so she didn't waste any time getting to her point. I don't remember any greeting or small talk, only that she asked if I planned on substitute teaching.

It caught me slightly off guard because I knew God was leading me to write. I also knew that if I were to substitute teach almost every day, I wouldn't have time to do anything else. In my mind, I still struggled with how to proceed and tried to explain that I couldn't sub without a physical or TB test. She said, "So, you're not in any hurry to sub?" The word *hurry* carried more weight than it might seem.

I tried to be respectful and explained that I hadn't realized I needed another TB test and mentioned my belief that God wanted me to write and how I was learning all I could about blogging. Without missing a beat, she said, "Or at least that's what you're going to pursue."

Ouch.

Because I didn't want to argue with her, I let it drop and didn't try to defend myself or my decisions. I wish I could say it was the last time she would push me to choose a different path, but it wasn't. We had the same back and forth conversation that next summer. Even though I knew God was pleased with my words to her, I was sad and stressed not to have the answers she wanted. More than anything, I wanted to know God's plans for me. Maggie didn't seem concerned with whether or not I obeyed God, only that I would be doing something to produce immediate income.

The next day, I was still dealing with the after-effects of that encounter. As I paced the hallway, I began to pray out loud to God about how unfair it was that I had to go through this over and over again. He reminded me of Jesus and all He went through for me. I knew my sufferings were trivial in comparison, but God lovingly spoke Psalm 56:8 to me. I had no idea what it said, so I looked it up: "Record my misery; list my tears on your scroll—are they not in your record?"

I knew God had heard me, and in my journal I wrote, "God is listening to me."

Friend, let me assure you: God sees you. He sees your pain and your tears, and He understands. Jesus went through far more than most of us ever will because of His love for you and me.

Can God rescue us from every situation? Yes, of course, but without testing to see what is in our hearts, we would never mature in our faith. James 1:2–4 says, "Consider it pure joy, my brothers and sisters, whenever you face trials of many kinds, because you know that the testing of your faith produces perseverance. Let perseverance finish its work so that you may be mature and complete, not lacking anything."

If we are going to live for Jesus in a world that doesn't know Him, we will experience pushback and more. We have to learn to stand up under pressure. But God is watching, and we can be sure anything that impacts our lives must be allowed by Him.[3]

Is it fun?

No.

Is it necessary?

Yes.

What makes it even more difficult is when we are believing God for something but have not yet seen it. You may have no proof to offer anyone, but don't allow others' words or actions to cause you to quit. God rewards those who do not give up. Run to him. He is waiting to strengthen and encourage you as He did for me.

When our fear of people eclipses our fear of God, we are in the danger zone. Proverbs 29:25 (NLT) tells us that "fearing people is a dangerous trap," and I think it's one of Satan's greatest weapons against us. I love the way The Message reads: "The fear of human opinion disables; trusting in GOD protects you from that" (Proverbs 29:25 MSG).

When we focus on people, it can immobilize us, but when we focus on God, it enables us to move forward.

No one can stop God's plans for your life. *No one.*

Fear saps our energy, steals our life, renders us ineffective, and causes us to focus on the enemy more than we focus on the One who has the power. What does this say about our relationship with God?

When Tony and I stood before God and our family and friends and promised to always love, cherish, and be faithful to each other for the rest of our lives, we meant it then, and we mean it today.

What would it say about our relationship if we doubted the goodness in each other?

And yet, we do this to God, don't we? When we choose to fix our eyes on the threats against us instead of on the One who will never leave us or forsake us, it shows that we really don't believe God is good, and we really don't believe He is all-powerful.

In Isaiah 54:17, we read, "'No weapon forged against you will prevail, and you will refute every tongue that accuses you.

This is the heritage of the servants of the LORD, and this is their vindication from me,' declares the LORD."

God is fighting for you *every day*.

However, if you are looking for everyone around you to understand and support you, you will be disappointed because everyone thinks they know what you should do.

While it's good to consider thoughts from trusted individuals, God may not be speaking to them about you, so you need to be careful.

The mind is a battleground, and it feels like the enemy always launches some kind of assault. The pressure of Maggie's words only intensified any feelings of doubt that the enemy continued to plant in my mind. Although I knew I wouldn't turn back, I still fought to focus on what God told me to do rather than focus on worldly wisdom, which says to follow the money.

As I struggled with these thoughts, one day, the Holy Spirit brought Psalm 39 to my mind. As I opened my Bible and read, verses five and six caught my eye: "You have made my days a mere handbreadth; the span of my years is as nothing before you. Everyone is but a breath, even those who seem secure. Surely everyone goes around like a mere phantom; in vain they rush about, heaping up wealth without knowing whose it will finally be."

He said, "Don't focus on the money. Life is shorter than you think. Focus on me and do what I am asking you to do."

God is fighting for you every day.

Are you a people pleaser or a God pleaser? How
does this affect the decisions you make?
Have the opinions or pressures exerted from others affected
your confidence in God and His plans for you? How
have you handled difficult situations? What truth about
God do you focus on to override any doubt or fear?

Chapter Eight
SWEET DREAMS

I will never forget the first time I realized God was speaking to me. No longer did my time with Him seem like something I had to check off my to-do list. Instead, it made me want to draw closer to Him, and He met me where I was. The abstract became tangible and forever changed the way I viewed our relationship.

God wants to speak with each and every one of us. I think the question then becomes if we will hear and understand. The Bible tells us that "God does speak—now one way, now another—though no one perceives it" (Job 33:14). What if God were speaking directly to you, but you were simply unaware?

We can talk to God anytime, anywhere, and He can speak to us anytime, anywhere, and in any number of ways, including through His word,[1] through the Holy Spirit,[2] messages or encouragement delivered through other people,[3] through creation,[4] in dreams,[5] or in visions.[6] Some have even heard God's voice out loud,[7] while others have seen angels.[8] We read examples in the Bible and listen to accounts from people today.

One of my former Sunday school students shared a story of waking up in the middle of the night and seeing an angelic glow cast onto a wall at the foot of the staircase in his home.

He said he was not frightened, did not question its presence, and casually mentioned it to his mother the next morning at breakfast. Having prayed about specific things, his mother felt the angel was there in response to her prayers. But what I found interesting was that the young man was the one who saw the angel and reported it to his mother.

God's presence and work in our lives are never-ending. He wants to communicate with each one of us, but the way He does this seems to vary from person to person.

As parents, we often tuck our children into bed at night with the words, "Sweet dreams." Most of the time, we don't really think much about it. But what if our dreams aren't always the product of our minds? What if they are actually encounters with the living God?

That fall, as I pressed in and focused on building my relationship with God, I realized that He was speaking to me in dreams. I don't know how to explain it, except that I was keenly aware that something was different than it had been before, and I was paying attention. Dreams that I knew were not simply from my subconscious mind spoke to the fact that God had work for me to do, and it was time to get started. I discovered that some dreams warned, while others encouraged or even spoke to the future.

One particular night, Tony was away on a business trip, and I found myself staring up at the ceiling, the hours ticking away. As morning approached, I finally fell back to sleep and dreamed that I was in a car with several other people, driving downtown into the business district of a city. I could see people walking toward a building on their way to work and a lounge chair moving by its own power toward the buildings, and it was carrying a briefcase. When I saw it, I was slightly amused and said, "Phoning it in."

I woke up to the chime of my phone as Tony texted, "Good morning, love."

SWEET DREAMS

After a quick text back, I called to tell him about my dream. It was so unlike any other dream I'd ever had, and I wondered what it meant.

I opened up my Facebook app, scrolled through my feed, and saw the link to a blog post titled "At the End of Myself" by Sagan Hundley. I clicked on the link and read the article. The author advised readers to get out of their "own head[s]" and allow God to define them.[9] She concluded with a quote from Oswald Chambers: "Get to the end of yourself where you can do nothing, but where He does everything."[10] In other words, we need to rest in God and give Him complete control of our lives.

I thought about my dream and the words I had read and knew God was telling me He had work for me to do. In my journal next to all of these things, I wrote: "I think God is telling me to get busy, write, and publish." I knew I would need to rest in Him, let the Holy Spirit lead me, and not worry about things that didn't really matter.

Later in the day, I heard the following words in my mind: "*Without Me you can do nothing.*"[11]

My dreams continued over the next few weeks and months. In the first one, I saw people who were in danger or needed help. But it was not like an ordinary, movie-like dream. Instead, it consisted of three short scenes, and as one scene ended, I found myself in the next one.

The second dream also contained several scenes. In the first one, Tony walked beside me down the stairway of an ancient building. The word "ruins" comes to mind. I saw other people on either side of me. Broken glass littered the steps and poked my feet because I was barefoot. When I got to the bottom of the stairs, I found something like a narrow piece of cloth and a pair of flip-flops (sandals) waiting for me. I wrapped my right foot with the piece of cloth and put on the sandals.

As the scene ended, I immediately found myself in the second scene. In this one, Tony and I stood on some ascending steps, which led to the doorway of a building. In my mind, it was a place of employment. I looked at Tony and asked, "Why are you going in there?" And he said, "You know why."

Just as quickly as that scene ended, I found myself in the third scene. Tony and I stood in the middle of a city, and it was dark. He handed me a set of keys, and I walked back across the city by myself.

As soon as I woke up, I immediately thought about how I would never walk across a city all by myself in the middle of the night. But in my dream, I was not afraid.

I have learned that in heavenly inspired dreams, one's husband can represent himself or God or Jesus.[12] In *most* of my dreams, I believe Tony functions as my loving husband. But this dream didn't feel like an ordinary dream.

Though I wrestled with how to explain this, the Bible refers to God as Israel's "husband" in Isaiah 54:5. We see Jesus as the "bridegroom" in Matthew 25:1–13, and He says, "I will give you the keys of the kingdom of heaven" in Matthew 16:19. In this specific dream, I believe this is who Tony represented. He was beside me as I walked down the stairway of the ancient building. I believe the ancient building represented the past,[13] and descending the stairway probably represented a loss of faith or spiritual strength.[14] The broken glass symbolized the enemy's attempts to bring fear and destruction, and I was unprepared to stand strong because I was not wearing sandals (shoes), which represent the "Gospel of peace."[15]

I believe that God was reminding me of my identity in Christ. At times, we may forget who we are as God's children. Because of what Jesus did on the cross for us, we have forgiveness of sin and peace with God. When the enemy launches an attack, we can stand firm, in peace, because we know God's power works in and through us, and the battle has already been won.[16]

Wrapping my foot may have represented a binding up (strengthening) because of sustained *injuries* from the enemy's past assaults.[17] Preparing to ascend the steps meant that the Holy Spirit would provide strength as I stepped into the work God had prepared for me.[18] I would also receive the keys ("authority") to carry out His will.[19] Though walking through darkness, God's power to help and protect me prevented any fear.

Through the years, I have had many other dreams. Some have spoken about things that would later happen, including moves and job changes. Prophetic dreams are biblical, and although God may not always reveal things before they happen, He can and does according to His will.

I have found that it's helpful to record my dreams in a journal, so I write down as many details as I can remember. There is often significance in the details and how or what I am thinking or feeling at the time.[20]

Interpreting dreams can be challenging. Some are more direct and easier to understand,[21] while others may contain symbolic imagery.[22] The Bible provides examples of both. God spoke to people through dreams. I have prayed and asked God to give me wisdom and understanding to interpret my dreams, talked to others who have prophetic dreams, and consulted books from Christian authors.[23] Searching the scriptures for symbolic imagery and its meaning can also help us to understand. God has surprised me in this way. His word is full of treasure and new points of discovery.

Sometimes, we understand the meaning, but at other times, we gain understanding as we pray for guidance or as we begin to see things happen around us.

As with other spiritual matters, it requires faith and humility. We may misunderstand because we are human and prone to mistakes, especially as we learn to discern new things.

I don't pretend to be an expert on this topic, but I do wholeheartedly believe God still speaks in this way.

CREATED FOR THE EXTRAORDINARY

In the last days, God says, I will pour out my Spirit on all people. Your sons and daughters will prophesy, your young men will see visions, your old men will dream dreams. Even on my servants, both men and women, I will pour out my Spirit in those days, and they will prophesy.

Acts 2:17–18

If any of you lacks wisdom, you should ask God, who gives generously to all without finding fault, and it will be given to you.

James 1:5

And without faith it is impossible to please God, because anyone who comes to him must believe that he exists and that he rewards those who earnestly seek him.

Hebrews 11:6

God gives knowledge and instruction about certain things, to certain people, at certain times, for specific purposes.

For the LORD gives wisdom; from his mouth come knowledge and understanding.

Proverbs 2:6

Trust in the LORD with all your heart and lean not on your own understanding; in all your ways submit to him, and he will make your paths straight.

Proverbs 3:5–6

Why would God choose to give us a particular message or show us something in the future? Perhaps it's to teach, warn, encourage, or prompt us to pray. At other times, it may be so we can be on the lookout for something to come, so when it happens, we will recognize that it's from Him. When I see evidence of my dreams, it reminds me that God is in control,

He knows what the future holds, and He is taking care of me. But I also believe the enemy can influence our dreams. (I talk more about this in Chapter 11.)

I know one thing for sure: I don't have all the answers. But I have learned to ask God to help me understand what He is trying to teach me.[24] This is why spiritual discernment is so important. We have to know God and understand His character. The best way we can do this is to read the Bible, spend time with Him, and pray for wisdom. God would never instruct us to do something that is contradictory to His word. If your message goes against what He says in the Bible, you can be certain that it's not a directive from Him. God would never instruct us to sin.

Maybe you've never experienced a God-inspired dream. If so, please understand that it doesn't mean you don't have a strong relationship with God. As of the writing of this book, I can't say that I have ever seen an angel in person (at least that I know of). However, I know others have had this experience. If you desire for God to speak to you in a particular way, I encourage you to pray about it. You never know, He may just surprise you.

On the Friday after Thanksgiving, we went to our family's farm for target practice—a family tradition. I stood in the middle of the pasture with gunfire around me, but my thoughts were with God, as I talked to Him about how much I often felt like an outsider. My path looked so different from everyone else's, and even though I knew God had ordained my next steps, I still felt *less than* because not everyone understood what God was doing in my life. To some, it looked like I wasn't doing anything of value, and I couldn't provide more information because I still didn't know what God had up His sleeve.

As I prayed about these things, Psalm 21 flashed into my mind along with the word "higher." I pulled out my phone, looked up Psalm 21 in my Bible app, and read verses one and two: "The king rejoices in your strength, LORD. How great is his joy in the victories you give! You have granted him his heart's desire and have not withheld the request of his lips."

In the verses that follow, the psalmist details how God blessed the king because he trusted his Lord to defeat his enemies. God said to me, "Trust me. Think higher. The world has its ways, but 'my ways [are] higher,'[25] and I will provide for you and help you do what I have called you to do."

That December, I began to write and publish on my blog again. To my surprise, I received a note from one of my readers. In the letter, this woman said she didn't understand why, but my writing had struck a nerve. She went on to say that she didn't know if she would ever believe the same way I did but hoped that I would continue to write.

I sent a note thanking her for her kind words. She could never have known how much I needed to hear them, but God did. He allowed me to see that I could make a difference in someone's life and reminded me that there is always a reason for the things He asks us to do, even if we don't understand it at the time. When you don't understand but remain determined in your heart to obey, He may use you in ways you never even imagined possible to impact the lives of others for His kingdom.

God wants to communicate with you.

In what way(s) does God communicate with you?
What message do you believe He is speaking to you today?

Chapter Nine
OUT OF MY COMFORT ZONE

It was 4:30 on a Friday afternoon, and Tony called from the office to ask if I would like to see the 5:00 p.m. showing of *Rogue One: A Star Wars Story*. It had been out for almost three weeks, and we still had not seen it.

We chose seats one row up from the main floor. Two men and one woman sat in front of us. The woman wore the most interesting spectacles that I had ever seen—the lenses flipped up or down. Tony and I both noted how unique they were.

After we watched the movie for a while, I looked down at the trio and heard in my mind, *Go talk to those people.* I thought, *Lord, did you really just tell me to talk to those people? I don't know them. What would I say? You know, they might think I'm crazy.* I even entertained the thought that it was only my imagination.

Perhaps God had not asked me to do such a thing—at least I hoped not—so I continued to debate the issue in my mind, reminding God why it didn't make any sense.

As the movie ended and the credits rolled, I was ready to leave, but Tony always likes to watch them until the very end to make sure the film's producers didn't add a comedic outtake or blooper. So, we sat there and watched the list run down the screen.

I leaned over and pleaded with a laugh, "Come on. We're on the list of accountants now."

He laughed and said, "Just wait."

It was Tony and me, the trio below, and another couple behind us. Everyone else had left the theater.

As the trio prepared to leave, they moved to the end of the aisle and paused for a few moments. Tony and I stood up, and I moved toward the exit, hoping he would follow.

Gently nudging him one last time, I said, "Come on; it's over." He took one last drink of his iced tea, stepped down, and looked toward the darkened floor. Bending down, he picked up a hat and gloves and asked the lady, "Do these belong to you?"

She said, "Oh, yes, and is there a scarf too?" He picked up a scarf as well and handed it to her. She thanked him, and we went on our way.

As we drove home, I told him about what I had heard and my struggle to follow through. I said, "God spoke to me and said to talk to them, but you did what He told me to do. How did you even see the hat, gloves, and scarf? It was dark."

He said, "I'm just observant."

Tony had not heard the words. He had only seen a need and tried to help. I had heard the words but had not seen the need. How many times do we miss God's voice because we are in too big of a hurry to notice what He has orchestrated for us? How often do we ignore it because we doubt it's from him or brush it off because it's something we would rather not do?

I am not very comfortable with walking up to total strangers without a good reason and had no idea why I needed to talk to them or what I was supposed to say.

Looking back, I realized I didn't need to come up with the perfect words. If I had waited, I would have had the opportunity to say hi, and perhaps I would have noticed their missing items. I thought it was all on me rather than taking a step of faith and allowing God to do the rest.

Later, as I processed everything, I realized one or more of the following things had taken place:

- God proved to me that I had, indeed, heard His voice. Maybe that was His goal all along.

- Maybe Tony's discovery of the lost items was the introduction I needed to do what God had asked me to do.

- Perhaps God used it as a teaching moment so the next time He instructs me to talk to a total stranger, I will understand how to proceed.

The request was simple, but I had made it so much bigger in my mind. God doesn't expect us to have all the answers. But He does expect us to do what He asks us to do, and He will take care of the rest.

My sheep listen to my voice; I know them, and they follow me.
John 10:27

What is God asking you to do that is outside of your comfort zone?

It was the beginning of a new year, a year that would challenge me in multiple ways, preparing me for all that God was planning to do in my life.

Go!

It was the third week of January 2017, and I called my mom to wish her a happy birthday. During our conversation, I shared that I had asked people in my online prayer group to pray for my dad's health issues. I also told her God was doing amazing things in my life, and I believed writing would be just one piece of everything He had planned for me.

After listening, she said a lady in her women's group had asked about me and wondered if I would speak about prayer at their church's women's prayer breakfast sometime in the next few months. The women were going to be reading *Anything* by Jennie Allen.

I told her I wanted to pray about it first but that I would say yes because I believed God had speaking in mind for me. I just didn't think it would be so soon. It excited and terrified me all at the same time, but I knew if God had called me to do it, He had already equipped me and would give me everything to see it through.

We settled on a date a couple of months away, and I began to write the message God had given to me. I knew He wanted me to encourage His people to take hold of His power that is available to us, but we are sometimes too blind to see. This blindness causes us to seek the wrong things and live a powerless life. There is so much that God wants to teach us, but we have to listen for His voice. I asked His Spirit to come alive in me, speak to me, and lead me. With open eyes, we need to see His power at work in us.

I remembered Him giving me verses when we lived in Iowa about "declar[ing] his glory" (Psalm 96:3) and "set[ting] the oppressed free" (Isaiah 58:6), but at the time, I didn't *really* understand what He was asking me to do, and I had *my* agenda. This time was different. I asked Him to fan into flame the gifts that He wanted me to possess.

A few days after speaking with my mom, I dreamed that a lady said to me, "Jesus is coming back tomorrow." I looked at her and asked, "How do you know?"

That was it—just one scene.

Tomorrow often means *future*.[1]

The next morning, as I scrolled through my Facebook feed, I saw a photo from Anne Graham Lotz, and on the photo were these words: "Be Ready to Meet Jesus."[2] I knew this was no coincidence. God's message to me was coming through loud and clear: Don't delay in doing what I've called you to do. Time is shorter than you think.

Challenged in St. Louis

Jennie Allen's "Nothing to Prove" tour took place in February throughout the Midwest, and Tony and I went to St. Louis to hear her speak. The auditorium was full of women, and Tony was one of only a few men in the audience during the main session. Afterward, when I had the opportunity to meet Jennie and have her sign my book, I told her about my invitation to speak at the Women's Prayer Breakfast at the church where I grew up.

She looked at Tony and me and said, "Have you guys prayed that prayer ('God we will do anything. *Anything.*')?"[3]

I said, "Yes, I think so. I'm really trying. Your books have really impacted me."

As we walked to the car, her question lingered in my mind. I wanted to mean it but wondered if I was truly there yet. Although I knew I was on the right path to write and speak and felt at peace with those things, her words caused me to wonder what else it might mean. I didn't know what was ahead. What if I wasn't okay with it? Tony and I hadn't yet prayed the prayer as a couple.

Days later as I sat in front of my fireplace, her question crept back into my mind, and I wondered, *What might God do if we prayed the prayer together? Would anything in our lives change? And if so, what?*

The next couple of months flew by as spring approached. God continued to prepare my heart and mind with encouraging verses like Isaiah 57:14: "Build up, build up, prepare the road! Remove the obstacles out of the way of my people." I prepared for my first speaking engagement, excited to share everything that God had been doing in my life with the ladies at my hometown church.

Eight days before I was supposed to speak, I tested positive for influenzas A and B. I couldn't get just one kind of flu—it had to be both kinds. Although I'd never had a flu shot before, I had only had the influenza virus (the kind that knocks you off your feet) once that I could remember.

I texted my mom about the possibility of rescheduling. It seemed that it would be best for them to find another speaker for the day. They agreed there might be more to share in the months to come, so we should wait.

That same month, after five weeks of symptoms, I learned that I had a uterine fibroid. My visit to the gynecologist's office ended with an unplanned biopsy. So many things circled inside my head. The tissue samples showed no trace of cancer, so I was advised to have regular checkups to ensure nothing changed.

The attacks on my body continued. I felt terribly ill for three to four hours after small group one evening—my stomach and intestines hurt. I felt hot then cold and shook. On our way home from a conference in Chicago, I felt sick again as we waited to board the flight. I texted family and friends and asked them to pray for me, and not long after our flight took off, I finally felt better.

April was a rough month, and as I reflected on two dreams I'd had in March, I believed God was trying to warn me about some spiritual warfare attacks. In the first dream, I went from room to room in a house. Some doors were closed; others were open. But snakes were everywhere. I stepped toward one closed door, and before I opened it, two small snakes and one large one emerged from under the door. As I moved away to another room where the door was already open, there were more snakes.

A few weeks later, I dreamed that I was in an open field in the center of a circle comprised of doorways several feet apart. There were other people in the circle with knives and swords. They seemed to think it was a game to throw them at me. I wanted to leave and tried to make it to one of the doorways, but they attempted to prevent me from escaping. Miraculously, I was unharmed. I believe these dreams represented the enemy's attempts to keep me from the opportunities that God was bringing before me.[4]

Four days before the women's prayer breakfast, I heard in my spirit, *Go!* I believe it was God's affirmation of my mission to tell others about the wonderful things He was doing in my life and confirmation that I was on the right path and moving forward in all He was preparing for me.

I felt such peace amid all my other emotions as I arrived at the church that Saturday morning. Something was so right about my first speaking engagement taking place at my childhood church. God had brought me back to the beginning to prepare me for what my future had in store. I will never forget the experience. It was so personal, the women so gracious and affirming, and I teared up while telling my story of surrender. A little embarrassed, I apologized, but one very kind lady said, "It's okay. It's just the Holy Spirit."

My time with those wonderful ladies solidified my desire to speak and share with others what I knew the Lord was teaching me. Less than a couple of weeks later, I texted my friend Kristy with these words: "My calling, I believe, is to inspire others to take hold of God's power in their lives and follow His calling—to [help] 'remove the obstacles'[5]—and my experiences while learning to do that in my own life are part of the message I have to give."

God's plans will often require you to step outside of your comfort zone.

In what way is God calling you to step outside of your comfort zone?

Chapter Ten
YES, NO, WAIT

We need to trust God with everything because He is the only one who truly knows what is best for us and what our future holds. Like an earthly parent, His answers for His children will fall into one of the following categories: yes, no, or wait. As adults, we are very much like our children—we want to have our own way, don't we?

But over the years, I have learned that God's "thoughts" and "ways" are "higher" than mine (Isaiah 55:8–9). Although the Bible tells me this concept is true, I have also seen the outcomes of waiting on Him and the good that comes from obeying Him instead of going my own way in life.

It brings us great joy when God gives us exactly what we want, but how well do we handle things when we don't receive what we have asked for or have to wait and wonder?

God Directs the Rhythms of Life

God is always at work, even in our disappointments. If we believe that God is in control and must allow whatever comes into our lives, then we must trust Him in everything.

Disappointments serve to redirect our focus and our steps.

When I was a teenager, I applied for several jobs in the town where I lived. Secretly, I hoped to work at a small variety store, partly because the hours were better. They closed relatively early in the evening, which meant that I could get home and still have time to relax and do homework before bed on weekdays or meet friends after work on the weekends. However, the store was not hiring.

Instead, I received a call from the pizza restaurant in town. It wasn't my first choice because it stayed open until 11:00 p.m. on weeknights and midnight on weekends. Closing those nights meant an additional hour of clean up after closing, which meant getting home late. But I needed a job, and it was the only place that had offered me one.

I didn't know it at the time, but I would meet my future husband there, so I am thankful that I didn't get the job I thought I wanted.

Tony was hired at the restaurant one month before me. I wasn't looking for a boyfriend before I started, but he very quickly made an indelible impression on me. He made the most mundane tasks fun—like when we played basketball with a ball of pizza dough in the back of the kitchen.

My mom used to say, "You could sit Tony on a chair in the middle of the room, not give him anything else, and he would find a way to have fun." He has continued to bring joy and adventure into my life for many years.

In His wisdom, God knew His plans for me—plans that would impact the rest of my life. I am so glad I trusted Him enough to say yes, even when I didn't know what was ahead. I couldn't imagine my life without Tony and our children, our son-in-law, and our granddaughters. Well, you get the picture. God is good, and His plans for us are for our good and His glory. In everything, we have to remember—we can trust Him.

When Opportunity Knocks

While I waited for a mentor and for God to show me how I was supposed to get my writing in front of a publisher, my podcasting interest grew. Podcasts were a growing trend, and the more I listened to some of my favorite people, the more I thought it would be exciting to team up with someone else, interview people, and talk about fun topics.

Although I had never met Meredith in person, we had spoken on the phone a few times, and I thought I might be able to learn a few things from her. So, I sent her a message to ask what she knew about podcasting.

When I didn't hear back a few nights later, my mind began to process some concerns. Prayerfully, I asked God why I didn't have peace when I thought about partnering with her, even though she had broached the subject of the two of us working together before. In my spirit, I heard God speak and knew the answer was no.

A little over twelve hours later, she responded and said that she had considered doing a podcast, too, and that we could talk about possibly doing one together. She said, "Ultimately, no matter what you do, you need an audience. More than that, you need an *interested* audience, which can take time."

The next morning, I prayed about God's words, her message, and my lack of peace. The Holy Spirit put the following scriptures into my mind. As He spoke, I looked them up and wrote them down. It was a back-and-forth conversation, and this is what I heard:

> *LORD, you establish peace for us; all that we have accomplished you have done for us.*
>
> Isaiah 26:12

I knew that we should experience peace when moving within the will of God, even if the road is not an easy one. But I didn't feel peace.

> *I make known the end from the beginning, from ancient times, what is still to come. I say, "My purpose will stand, and I will do all that I please."*
>
> Isaiah 46:10

I knew that He was in control, not me, and that His plans would come to pass.

I said, *Lord, are you telling me that you have already set other plans into motion for me and that this opportunity (even though it sounds good) is not your will for me?*

He responded:

> *In their hearts humans plan their course, but the LORD establishes their steps.*
>
> Proverbs 16:9

With these words, I understood the message to be, "You have one thing in mind, but I determine what you will do."

So, I had my answer.

When we are aligned with God's will, we will have peace, and I didn't have it for partnering with Meredith on the podcast. But I knew God would present me with plans He had already put into place, and I needed to remain in faith.

Although I understood, His *no* put me in a waiting space again. Waiting can be a no, but not always. Sometimes, it means that it's not yet the right time. When we keep our minds focused on Him and His goodness, we hold the key to maintaining the right attitude and not slipping into a mindset of fear and doubt. One of the best ways to do this is to praise Him in our waiting.

Have you ever felt sad or uninspired and then turned on some music that ministered to your soul? Music speaks to us. I feel God's presence and become energized when I'm listening to praise songs. It puts my focus back where it should be.

> *The trumpeters and musicians joined in unison to give praise and thanks to the LORD. Accompanied by trumpets, cymbals and other instruments, the singers raised their voices in praise to the LORD and sang: 'He is good; his love endures forever.' Then the temple of the LORD was filled with the cloud, and the priests could not perform their service because of the cloud, for the glory of the LORD filled the temple of God.*
>
> 2 Chronicles 5:13–14

Praise Him in the waiting. God is always at work, even when we cannot see what He is doing.

> *As they began to sing and praise, the LORD set ambushes against the men of Ammon and Moab and Mount Seir who were invading Judah, and they were defeated.*
>
> 2 Chronicles 20:22

When we stay connected to God and remember that nothing happens by accident, we can remain in faith even when things around us begin to shift. Possessions, opportunities, jobs, even friendships may only be with us for a season, but God and His plans will be with us forever.

How does this understanding help us?

Well, it enables us to let go of anything we perceive as a disappointment. It encourages us to remain steadfast in the knowledge that God already has our days planned out for us. Practically speaking, the possessions, opportunities, jobs, and friends that God knows you need will come to you, which is all we need to know.

Think Anew

As summer came to an end and fall approached, Tony and I took a walk on the campus of Kansas State University. I noticed a sign on the wall of the Marianna Kistler Beach Museum of

Art: "Think Anew." I talked with Tony about how everything was new for me. I understood that I needed to do things God's way, and even though there may be any number of *good* things I could do, I believed God had something specific in mind for me, and I needed to be careful to follow His voice.

My mind processed everything differently as He continued to renew it and help me align my thoughts with His thoughts. There's such peace when you realize what is happening and decide to allow God to move in and through you.

Two nights later, I had a dream that I boarded a large bus and fastened my seat belt. I knew this meant something because nearly a year earlier, I'd had another dream in which I learned that a bus was coming, and I was supposed to be on it, but I missed it because I wasn't ready. This dream represented that I was finally on board and moving toward my "destiny" (what God was calling me to do).[1]

A few weeks later, I went with Tony to West Des Moines for meetings. God was energizing me to write, and I knew my changed way of thinking was part of the story He wanted me to share with others.

As we sat in the hotel's snack bar area with some of his colleagues, a woman struck up a conversation with me, asking me questions about my line of work. I had struggled with answering this question before, but this time was different. Instead of saying I wanted to be a writer, as usual, I told her I was working on a project.

Thank goodness she didn't ask me twenty questions—I was only beginning and had little idea of what it could become. However, I knew what to do, and it was the first time I stated it out loud. It was the start of this book, which I had begun in my hotel room right before the conversation. I knew, in that moment, everything was about to change.

To step out in faith, I asked some of my closest friends to pray for me as I wrote. I would like to say that it was smooth sailing and that the battles end when you obey God, but the enemy didn't make it easy on me. Almost as soon as I began, I struggled with clarity and the desire to continue. I knew it wasn't normal, but you can understand that you are in a spiritual battle and still not feel like you can do anything about it.

I hadn't truly learned how to fight yet, but God was getting ready to show me how. When you set your eyes on beginning and finishing your race, the enemy will wage battle after battle against you because he has no intention of allowing you to complete your mission. If he cannot stop you in your tracks, he will try to frustrate you.

You may be thinking, *This doesn't sound fun at all. What's the point?*

It isn't fun. It's not meant to be. But if you keep moving forward, one step at a time, and never give up, you will learn to see good even in the difficulty.

Will you have bad days? Sure.

But let me share a little secret: Don't despise the battles. Stay faithful, pray, rest in Him, and watch expectantly. During this time, you may see Him do the most wonderful things on your behalf, even in the midst of the battle.

Angels All Around

I wish I could see God's angels in action. Years ago, during a difficult time, the Holy Spirit spoke the following words to me: *Walk as one who walks with God. No fear.* Those words reminded me that angels are around me, even when I cannot see them.

One of my favorite Old Testament stories is the one about Elisha and the Arameans (2 Kings 6:8–23). The King of Aram planned to attack Israel, but the prophet Elisha always warned the King of Israel ahead of time, so the Israelites were prepared.

The King of Aram suspected that one of his men had conspired with the Israelite army, but they assured him that this was not the case. It was Elisha who was aware of the King's plans and told the King of Israel. Thinking he could stop this prophet of God, the King of Aram found out where Elisha was staying and sent his men to apprehend him.

The next morning, one of Elisha's servants went out and saw that the Arameans had besieged the city and warned him. Elisha assured the servant that God was with them, and he didn't need to be afraid. "Elisha prayed, 'Open his eyes, LORD, so that he may see.' Then the LORD opened the servant's eyes, and he looked and saw the hills full of horses and chariots of fire all around Elisha."[2]

An army of God's angels stood guard and protected him. There wasn't even a battle that day. Elisha asked God to make the Arameans blind, then "he led them to Samaria," brought them before the King of the Israelites, and instructed that they be allowed to live.[3] The God-fearing hosts gave food to the Arameans and "sent them away," and the Arameans suspended their attacks on Israel.[4]

Elisha trusted God's power to deliver him from evil, and his servant received the ability to see God's horses and chariots of fire. I can only imagine how that would change someone.

Friend, God is watching over you and me. If we truly believed this, why would we fear anyone or anything?

I want to continually be aware of His presence in my life. Maybe we should pray like Elisha for God to open our eyes. Father, give us eyes to see.

God is working behind the scenes, even when you cannot see what is happening.

How do you handle waiting on God?
What are you trusting Him for right now?

Chapter Eleven
MEET ME IN LAS VEGAS

That fall, God impressed upon me that it was time to write. I didn't know how it would all come together and had prayed for a mentor—someone to show me how to accomplish the things God wanted me to do—for quite some time and wondered how and when to expect answers to my prayers.

Tony found out that he would be going to Las Vegas for a work trip, and I could go with him. I had never been to "Sin City" before but was excited for the opportunity to get away for a few days. In my prayers about our upcoming trip, I asked God to meet me there.

As the holidays approached, I felt anxiety begin to build inside of me when I thought of having to field questions about my writing when I still didn't have many answers. I didn't intend to mention it at our church small group meeting, but there in the circle, listening quietly to others' prayer requests, I felt God leading me to speak. It was as if the flood gates opened. I shared how I couldn't do what God had called me to do alone and how He had told me to say no to the only opportunity that had presented itself.

I was trying to trust God and not worry about others' opinions, but it was so hard and didn't feel fair. Tears welled up in my eyes as I talked.

My friend Dave reminded me to be salt to an unkind world. Although I knew his words were true, they didn't provide much comfort at the time. I was still waiting on God and had no idea how His timeline looked.

The only thing I knew for sure was that I wasn't going to turn back.

Not this time.

I wanted so badly to hear from God.

One week before our trip, I had three different dreams. In the first dream, I saw the face of author and publisher Kary Oberbrunner and was given two words to remember. But when I woke up, I couldn't remember the words, only that they began with an A and/or an R.

I didn't know what to think, so I didn't do anything. Although I knew of Oberbrunner because a friend had shared his name and program with me, I hadn't followed along with Author Academy Elite, so my dream was completely out of left field.

A couple of days later, I had a dream about a woman who was addressing a group of people, and I was also there. We were talking amongst ourselves rather than listening to the instructions. The woman walked toward me and handed me an illustration of some kind.

I asked, "Do you want me to give this to her?" referring to a small girl standing next to me, and she nodded. Then, I moved closer to hear what she was saying. However, there were others who were still not paying attention, so she led the group outside.

When I woke up, I asked God what He was trying to tell me. Immediately, the Holy Spirit led me to Isaiah 48:18–19.

> *If only you had paid attention to my commands, your peace would have been like a river, your well-being like the waves of the sea. Your descendants would have been like the sand,*

your children like its numberless grains; their name would never be blotted out nor destroyed from before me.

My message from this dream was to *pay attention*. The verses confirmed it, and the words suggested that there was much more riding on my action or inaction than I had ever realized.

A day or two later, I had a third dream. I was alone and about to ascend a staircase when a demonic figure (in human form) moved down the staircase toward me.

Terrified, I quietly uttered the words, "In Jesus' name, be gone."

I had to repeat it with more authority, so I said the words again in a louder voice. Upon my command, the figure threw herself over the staircase and landed on the floor below, no longer moving.

As I woke up and reflected, I understood God's lesson. My battle with spiritual oppression had led to that point, and I believe God may have allowed me to see what was happening in the spiritual realm as He prepared to open doors for me. I also believe He showed me that I had His power within me to overcome all that would come against me as I took on His work.

Though terrified in my dream, I stood my ground and prayed against the enemy in the name of Jesus. I believe this was a turning point in my life. Years earlier, I'd had a very different experience. There was about a two-year period when I believe a demonic entity harassed me in the night. At first, it always seemed to happen on a Friday, Saturday, or Sunday night, usually between midnight and 1:00 a.m. Although I had never talked in my sleep or faced torment by nightmares, during these encounters, I saw a tall, dark, faceless figure enter my bedroom and stand by the door. I woke up screaming and shaking, and Tony would have to calm me down. Toward the end, the figure appeared right beside my bed. I didn't understand what was happening and told very few people.

However, I did mention it to a friend after church one day, and she prayed over me. Tony also prayed for me as he comforted me, but it took my friend praying over me a second time before it stopped. To this day, I still don't know what happened or why. I have never been involved in the occult or anything that would knowingly put me at risk for the enemy's harassment.

I felt powerless to do anything about it during those two years, but much had happened since then. As I truly surrendered to God and asked for more of His Spirit in my life, I felt a shift. I believe He was preparing me to battle against the enemy so I wouldn't be a victim any longer. By His power, I would be victorious and teach others how to live in the Spirit so they could achieve victory in their lives as well.

The day before we left on our trip, I told my friend Kristy about my dreams. She said, "Kristi, Kary Oberbrunner is opening his program, Author Academy Elite. I think you should consider applying."

I had no idea that Oberbrunner's program was opening up, and I felt confident that I was not ready to write a book. Up until then, I had been calling what I was writing "my project." I had no idea what I would do with it. Perhaps it would turn into a Bible study or possibly a book, although I didn't know how to publish it. I only knew I was supposed to get it done, and I wasn't going to disappoint God again.

As we flew high above the clouds on our way to Las Vegas, I took a photo from my window seat. It looked out over the wing of our plane with beautiful, white clouds below.

After we landed, I posted the photo on my Facebook page along with the caption: "Soaring high above the clouds on our way to Las Vegas. The beauty of God's creation always inspires me." Seeing the post, Kristy commented, "Don't ever forget this moment! God met you there and is taking you to *new* heights!" I didn't realize it at the time, but those words carried more meaning than I had even realized.

In the weeks and months before our trip, I had knowingly battled spiritual oppression, and it rendered me nearly incapable of writing my project. My mind was cloudy, and I felt tired and distracted. I fought but didn't see the victory.

After the three dreams, something inside of me changed. I woke up the first morning in Las Vegas, confident in what God wanted me to do. As I prayed and asked Him to confirm His plans for me, the following verses flashed into my mind:

> *Commit to the LORD whatever you do, and he will establish your plans.*
>
> Proverbs 16:3

> *In God we make our boast all day long, and we will praise your name forever.*
>
> Psalm 44:8

> *Burst into songs of joy together, you ruins of Jerusalem, for the LORD has comforted his people, he has redeemed Jerusalem.*
>
> Isaiah 52:9

As I read through Isaiah 52, two words stood out to me.

> **Awake**, *awake, Zion, clothe yourself with strength! Put on your garments of splendor, Jerusalem, the holy city. The uncircumcised and defiled will not enter you again.*[1] *Shake off your dust;* **rise** *up, sit enthroned, Jerusalem. Free yourself from the chains on your neck, Daughter Zion, now a captive.*[2]

I remembered that the dream where I saw Oberbrunner's face also contained one or two words, but all I could remember was an A and/or an R. As I read those verses, *awake* and *rise* up jumped out at me, and I knew God had confirmed that applying to Author Academy Elite was His plan for me.

Tony came back to the hotel room, and I told him that I knew God wanted me to apply to the program and that I needed to listen to a webinar and fill out the application. He said, "Let's go to the convention center and take in Cowboy Christmas, then you can spend the afternoon working on everything before our evening activities."

I am not a cowgirl, but Cowboy Christmas was so much fun. There were vendors for everything imaginable, and we even got to watch a live taping of a show for the network that was covering the National Finals Rodeo and interviewing participants. I felt like I was on cloud nine that day because I knew God was up to something. He had met me there and answered my prayers.

As we walked among the crowds of people in the Las Vegas Convention Center, I walked a little taller in my new black boots, literally and figuratively. I felt stronger and more confident, like a woman on a mission for God, a warrior princess of my King, and I was ready to kick some evil butt.

I am an over-preparer by nature, but in that moment, I felt very underprepared. It had not been my plan for one of the biggest moments of my life to happen on our trip. I didn't have any of my notes for my project with me, but when He says *go*, we have to go because He's God, and He's in control. We learn to trust Him in those moments, do our best, and allow Him to cover us in everything else.

When we returned to the hotel that afternoon, I watched the webinar, filled out the application, and explained my book's topic as best as I could. Tony came back before I had completed everything, so I retreated to a quiet space inside the bathroom—the only seat available—to finish. I finally hit the submit button and prayed that God would fill in any gaps left by my unpreparedness. I knew it was in His hands as Tony and I left for the National Finals Rodeo competition.

High up in our seats at the Thomas and Mack Center, I was officially at my first rodeo, and I was really impressed. The loud music played as we watched cowboys try to stay on the backs of bucking broncos, and I wondered how they would be able to walk the next day.

As we delighted in the sights and sounds of the evening, I took out my phone and checked my email. One stood out to me. It said AAE had reviewed my application, I had advanced to the next round, and I needed to schedule an interview in the next few days.

My excitement grew. *What if this was it? What if this was the moment I had been waiting for?*

When we got back to the hotel, I checked the available dates and times and scheduled my interview. It was a whirlwind of a Sunday two days later as we flew home. I used my time in the air to go over my notes and prepare. Even though our flight landed behind schedule, we got our luggage, found our car, and even stopped at Dunkin' Donuts to get some coffee and donut holes (brain fuel) before my 7:30 p.m. interview.

I was excited and nervous as I spoke with Niccie Kliegl over the phone and told her about my book's premise. She told me that she knew I was right for the program even before we talked but that she needed to hear me explain everything. Immediately after the interview, I received an email that invited me to be part of the program.

And just like that, my next adventure had begun.

This ordinarily cautious girl, who usually wants to approach things carefully, received a short window of opportunity to take a huge leap of faith, and I jumped because I knew God was behind it all. Did I *feel* ready? Not really, but God finishes anything He begins, and that knowledge gave me the confidence to bravely move forward.

I came home from Las Vegas tired, thankful, and amazed at everything God had put into motion in just a few days' time. My experience taught me that my willingness to pray for God to use me in big ways and my obedience—even when it doesn't make sense or seems out of reach—result in more adventures.

Don't be afraid, O land. Be glad now and rejoice, for the LORD has done great things.
Joel 2:21 NLT

**When you step out in obedient faith,
God will meet you there.**

Has God spoken to you about His plans for your life?
What opportunities has God placed before you?
How will you respond?

PART 3

Living the Adventure

Chapter Twelve
LIVING EACH DAY WITH INTENTION

Over the last five years, the Holy Spirit has impressed upon me a sense of urgency—life is short, Jesus is coming back again, and it may be sooner than we think.

How is your relationship with Jesus? Are you ready to meet Him face to face?

As I wrote this chapter, family members of several people Tony and I knew passed away. One was a young woman under the age of forty, one was a woman in her sixties, and one was a man in his eighties. My paternal grandmother lived to be 104 years old.

Statistics can only provide a rough estimate of how long each of us will live. The truth is that none of us knows when we will take our last breath and living an intentional life doesn't happen by accident.

Perhaps the Holy Spirit has whispered some new or old things to you. What will you do with those nudges? How do we make the most of our time here on this earth? How do we ensure that we can look back at the end of our lives with fewer regrets and a greater sense of knowing that we have lived our best life?

If we believe God is truly in control, orders our steps (Psalm 37:23 NKJV), and allows all that impacts our lives, it changes the way we look at everything. Each experience, then, must present an opportunity of some kind. Not everything is good, and we may never know why some things happen until we get to heaven and ask God. But we can trust in His sovereignty, knowing He loves us and has a good plan for our lives.

When we view life in this way, it shows God that we trust Him and keeps our eyes focused on Him instead of our circumstances. It's a healthier way to view the world around us and can help us experience joy even in difficult times. Here are some of the questions we can ask ourselves:

- What can/did I learn from this experience? What is God trying to teach me? (Patience: Maybe you learned to keep your cool and respond in a loving way when someone else wasn't so loving. Remember, our ultimate goal is to become more like Jesus.)

- What did I gain from this experience/encounter? (Perhaps you met someone new.)

- Did someone else gain from this experience? (Perhaps you were able to encourage or impact someone else's life for the better.)

Nothing can be out of control if God is in control. He never fails. He can't because He's God.

Take Control of Your Thoughts

Part of living an intentional life involves being intentional with what we allow to take up residence in our minds. Our thoughts matter.

Let's face it: Life is full of trials. People can be difficult to love, circumstances can seem unfair, and obstacles can appear too large—there are scary things in this world. But as Christians, we are commanded to "always be joyful" and "thankful," regardless of our situation (1 Thessalonians 5:16–18 NLT).

How is that possible?

Well, it doesn't mean that we have to *enjoy* or be *thankful* for bad circumstances. But we can be thankful for the hope we have in Jesus, who is with us in the midst of those circumstances and is over all things.

However, many times we allow negative thoughts to enter our minds and remain, stealing our joy and peace. Although it's not always easy, when we choose to focus on God and what is important to Him, He releases His power into our lives.

Are you waiting for a breakthrough?

Where is your focus most of the time—on God and what He can do in your life or on your problems?

We have all been there and understand what it's like to be fearful about things we can't control or don't understand. When we're not careful, those negative feelings can result in the inability to move forward with God's request. For some, it can even result in anxiety, depression, health issues, and bitterness.

But there is good news: We can choose to take control of our thoughts. Paul says, "Finally, brothers and sisters, whatever is true, whatever is noble, whatever is right, whatever is pure, whatever is lovely, whatever is admirable—if anything is excellent or praiseworthy—think about such things" (Philippians 4:8).

So how do we put this into practice?

- **Capture and Direct Each Thought**

Take captive every thought to make it obedient to Christ.
2 Corinthians 10:5

We have to be careful about what we allow to infiltrate our minds and consciously guard against the junk. When a negative thought occurs, we have the choice to dwell on it or to let it go.

The next time you find negative feelings begin to build in your mind, instead of phoning a friend to complain, decide to take back control of your thoughts and refocus them on Jesus. It may sound basic, but it's also really powerful.

- **Pray**

Prayer should be the first thing—rather than the last—we do because everything else has failed. *Do it immediately.* Take your concerns and present them to God. Allow Him to deal with your circumstances. He's the only one who knows what's going on and what needs to happen anyway, right?

- **Read the Bible**

Let God's word saturate your mind. I have found that when I feel anxious about anything, and I sit down and read His words, I begin to relax.

> *For the word of God is alive and active. Sharper than any double-edged sword, it penetrates even to dividing soul and spirit, joints and marrow; it judges the thoughts and attitudes of the heart.*
>
> Hebrews 4:12

His word is living, and it does work inside of us. The next time you are feeling anxious about anything, try it!

Oh friend, we are so blessed! Think about it: God is our provider.

> *And my God will meet all your needs according to the riches of his glory in Christ Jesus.*
>
> Philippians 4:19

God is our protector.

As for me, I call to God, and the LORD saves me. Evening, morning and noon I cry out in distress, and he hears my voice. He rescues me unharmed from the battle waged against me, even though many oppose me.
Psalm 55:16–18

God is our defender.

All who rage against you will surely be ashamed and disgraced; those who oppose you will be as nothing and perish. Though you search for your enemies, you will not find them. Those who wage war against you will be as nothing at all. For I am the LORD your God who takes hold of your right hand and says to you, Do not fear; I will help you.
Isaiah 41:11–13

God is the ultimate promoter.

It is God who judges: He brings one down, he exalts another.
Psalm 75:7

When we choose to take all things to God in prayer and focus on His word rather than worry, we gain the following benefits:

- We remember His faithfulness, regardless of our circumstances or our behavior, which produces joy.
- It keeps us within the will of God. We wait on Him instead of taking matters into our own hands because we know that His plans and timing are perfect.
- We get to live happier, peace-filled lives because our feelings are not subject to what others do or don't do.

God is *always* in control. Man is not. *Remember that.* For us, it means freedom to enjoy our lives, and it honors God.

Don't let Satan tell you there is no hope. If you have given your life to Jesus Christ, you have a God who fights for you. Trust Him.[1]

In the Old Testament, God instructed Moses to send some explorers to Canaan because He was going to give the land to the Israelites. Moses instructed them to investigate the towns and their inhabitants, the land, trees, soil, and even the fruit growing in the area. The men, including Joshua and Caleb, did as instructed and returned with fruit samples and a detailed report about the plentiful bounty of the land and the "powerful" inhabitants who lived in "fortified" cities.[2] Clearly, the explorers were amazed *and* terrified by what they saw.

Caleb said, "We should go up and take possession of the land, for we can certainly do it."[3] He knew if God had said He would give them the land, they didn't need to worry. They would be successful in the conquest. However, the other men who had gone to explore the land were fearful and alarmed the others with their words (Numbers 13).

Joshua and Caleb, part of the exploring expedition, were full of faith and tried to encourage them not to be afraid because God was with them, but the people were not convinced and "talked about stoning them."[4] God saw it all. He appeared to Moses and declared that none of the men who saw His miraculous deeds and still refused to obey His commands would ever see the promised land.

The Lord spared Joshua and Caleb, but the other men who explored the land and then incited the people to fear and unbelief "were struck down and died of a plague."[5] The rest of the unbelieving Israelites were not off the hook either. Even though Moses warned them not to disobey God and that God would not be with them if they went, they decided to go up to the "hill country" and take possession of the land.[6] Just as Moses had said, the inhabitants of the land attacked the Israelites, and they were defeated (Numbers 14).

Our thoughts matter because what we believe determines our actions. If we allow fear and unbelief to reign in our minds, it will be easier to disobey what God asks us to do. But if we take those kinds of thoughts "captive" (2 Corinthians 10:5) and decide to focus on God and His promises, it will be easier to respond in obedience.

At times, we may still feel afraid, but we need to train our minds to redirect our thinking and concentrate on what we know to be true—God is good. He is all-powerful, loves us, and is ultimately in control of everything that affects our lives. Focusing on Him will give us the strength to move forward.

My Experience with the Lady in the Hotel

Tony had business meetings out of town, and I went with him. It was our last morning there, and we planned on leaving at noon, so I decided to stay at the hotel and catch up on some reading. While I sat at the desk, a lady from housekeeping knocked at the door. I answered it and explained that we had arranged for a late checkout. She said, "That's okay" and left.

I went back to the desk to read again but had a passing thought that I needed to pray for her. In the previous days, I had thought of how many times we say we will pray for someone instead of praying right then and there *with* them.

With all of this fresh in my mind, even though God hadn't said, "Go find her and pray with her," I still wondered, *Can I pray for her, or do I need to pray with her?* I struggled in my mind with how to proceed and decided it was safer and less awkward to pray right where I was.

As I sat there in the comfort of my hotel room, the muted television suddenly came on really loud. I looked up and thought, *What just happened?* I grabbed the remote to turn it down and noticed that the volume had gone from zero to eleven. I said, "God, are you trying to tell me something?" I sat back down and asked Him how He wanted me to pray. The word *kids* flashed into my mind, so I prayed for any children she might have. But I still wondered if I was supposed to find her.

I got up and looked out the peephole in the door and didn't see her. And then I prayed, "Lord, if you want me to pray with her, bring her back to my door." I wanted to be brave. About ten minutes later, she knocked on the door again. *This is your opportunity* passed through my mind as I approached the door. When I opened it, I smiled, and she said while walking her cart backward down the hallway, "It's okay."

I said, "Are you sure?"

She replied, "It's okay."

Now, I didn't want to chase her down the hall because that would just be weird, so I closed the door but wondered if I had disobeyed God.

He had not commanded me to pray with her. But I had made the gesture and then, out of fear, decided not to follow through.

I felt like a failure for a few days, but when I relayed the story to Tony, he spoke faith into me by saying, "He's teaching you," and we talked about how I could handle a similar situation in the future. It probably would begin with, "I know this may sound crazy . . ."

God is patient with us, and He knows when we try to follow Him. He wants to teach us how to handle these things and will equip us if we cooperate with Him.

Being Spirit-led involves allowing God to interrupt our plans. We may have our day planned out and something unexpected happens, and we find our schedule has suddenly been altered. I think if most of us are honest, too often, our initial reaction is frustration. But what if God is inviting us to be part of something greater? God is usually full of surprises.

In Acts 8, we learn about Philip's experience with this very thing. The Bible tells us that an angel instructed Philip to go to a certain road. In obedience, Philip headed in that direction and along the way saw an Ethiopian eunuch riding in a chariot.

The Spirit directed Philip to approach the chariot. As he quickly moved closer, he "heard the man reading" from the book of Isaiah. Philip asked him if he understood the words he was reading, and the man replied, "How can I . . . unless someone explains it to me?"[7]

He "invited" Philip to ride with him in the chariot, and Philip began to tell the man the "good news about Jesus."[8] At some point during their conversation, they arrived upon some water, and the eunuch asked if he could be baptized, so "Philip baptized him." Then, "the Spirit of the Lord suddenly took Philip away" and the eunuch "went on his way rejoicing."[9]

I found this passage fascinating. An angel instructed Philip, and he obeyed even though he didn't know ahead of time why he'd received the instructions. He knew to *go*, and he went. Because of Philip's willingness to do what God asked him to do, another man received Jesus as his personal Lord and Savior.

I want to believe I could be so brave.

Just take off walking, Kristine.

No other instructions, Lord?

Just do what I am asking you to do. I will let you know more when the time comes.

Can you imagine?

Such surrender.

Such trust.

Such obedience.

God cannot use us if we are afraid to move when He tells us to move. He cannot use us if we are afraid to speak when

He tells us to speak. The good news is that He is patient, and He will work with us if our hearts are right before Him. I pray for more courage and want adventurous faith. How about you?

**Your thoughts matter because what you believe
and focus on will determine your actions.**

If you knew you only had one year to live, what
would you do with your last 365 days?
What priorities would be front and center?
What conversations would you have and with whom?
What things that now occupy your time
would no longer be important?

Are you allowing fear or faith to reign in your mind?
What thoughts do you need to take captive?
What truth about God do you need to focus on?

Chapter 13
PRAYING BOLD PRAYERS

Don't be someone who looks back over his or her life with regret and thinks, *I wish I would have known. If only I had trusted Him.* Friend, God is so real. Let me repeat it: God is so *real*. When you surrender to His plans for your life and spend more time getting to know Him and meet with Him in prayer, He will reveal more of Himself and His plans for your life to you.

There's nothing like it.

Whatever you find yourself going through, don't give up. God is more powerful than anything you may face. The enemy wants you to believe you are on your own, nobody will understand, there is no hope or solution, and your life will never be any different.

Don't listen to the lies of the enemy. You need to begin to speak the truth of God's word over your life and believe it.

I know that God is for me, so when I don't feel like praying, it's a good indication that's what I need to do. If we rely on feelings instead of following the Holy Spirit's promptings, we miss out and will never get to where God wants us to be. We need to live disciplined lives so we do the right thing even when the enemy gives us every excuse not to listen and obey.

God didn't intend for us to live defeated lives. The only way we can live in victory is by staying connected to the only one who has the power we need—Jesus.

What if we lived like we believe God is capable of doing anything?

What would our lives look like? What would our words sound like?

What actions would we take?

Our heavenly Father can change our circumstances in an instant. He can accomplish far more than you and I ever could in our strength and power alone. But we have to choose to trust Him.

He is the solution to all of life's problems.

Every single one.

Paul says to pray about everything and worry about nothing (Philippians 4:6–7). This means that we should bring all things before our heavenly Father—the small things, the big things, and everything in between. He wants to be involved in every aspect of our lives.

Asking shows faith.

You do not have because you do not ask God. When you ask, you do not receive, because you ask with wrong motives . . .
James 4:2–3

God knows what's in our hearts. He knows the reasons behind our prayers and if our thoughts are pure.

When you ask, do you believe?

Jesus said in Mark 9:23, "Everything is possible for one who believes." This indicates that faith (believing God can do anything according to His will) is an important part of seeing the power of God move in our lives.

Get God Involved Now

If you belong to Jesus, you have a heavenly Father who will take these burdens from you. Give them to Him.
How? you ask.

- Tell Him what is bothering you.
- Ask Him to intervene—to deal with the problems that are before you.
- Ask Him to show you what you need to do—if anything—and then do as He says. Remember, God will never ask you to do something that is against what the Bible teaches.
- Ask Him to give you His peace that "transcends all understanding" (Philippians 4:7).
- Do not let worry or fear take over your life.
- Don't give up. (See Daniel 10. Prayer is engaging in battle, and it affects things in the spiritual realm.)

The enemy wants you to focus on anything that distracts you from what God is doing in and around you, so when he puts a distraction into your mind, stop right where you are and give it to God.

Pray over the situation and trust that God will handle it. What Satan means for harm, God can turn around and use for good.

> *But Joseph said to them, 'Don't be afraid. Am I in the place of God? You intended to harm me, but God intended it for good to accomplish what is now being done, the saving of many lives.'*
>
> Genesis 50:19–20

God is always working on our behalf, even when we can't see what is happening. I want to pray bold prayers that are aligned with His will for my life and believe God for big things. I don't want to live a life that is so safe and secure that I don't have to trust Him. Do you? We need to be challenged so we can continue to grow and see His power at work. Father, give us your vision for our lives. Help us to see all that is possible with you.

Fasting for Breakthrough

Fasting is a spiritual discipline, and it often accompanies bold prayers. Most people find fasting to be a challenge because food is good. We need it to live, and it almost seems counter-intuitive to abstain from eating. Growing up, my only association with fasting was hearing someone recounting the negative physical effects of giving up food for a certain period of time.

Even now, we rarely discuss it in church, and I wonder why. We know God's people fasted in the Old Testament. Daniel fasted to humble himself before God, intercede on behalf of his people, and grow in knowledge and understanding (Daniel 1:11–17, 10). Esther fasted before she presented herself to King Xerxes in order to gain his favor, intervene on behalf of her people, and save them from destruction (Esther 4–8).

Jesus said, "And when you fast, do not look gloomy like the hypocrites, for they disfigure their faces that their fasting may be seen by others . . . But when you fast, anoint your head and wash your face, that your fasting may not be seen by others but by your Father who is in secret. And your Father who sees in secret will reward you" (Matthew 6:16–18 ESV).

Jesus' words "when you fast" suggest an assumption that one will do it. He doesn't say, "*if* you fast." Jesus fasted after His baptism when He was led into the wilderness by the Holy Spirit to be tempted by Satan (Luke 4:1–13).

But if we can just pray to God, why would we need to fast?

I believe fasting moves God's heart and better positions us to receive guidance and instruction from the Holy Spirit. When we are willing to deny those things that we would normally crave (whatever they might be), we humbly position ourselves before our heavenly Father and say, "I want You and Your will more than anything else."

Fasting and worship preceded the Holy Spirit's instruction to "set apart" and send out Saul (Paul) and Barnabas to preach the gospel (Acts 13:1–3).

But if fasting is so powerful, why don't we make it a regular part of our prayer lives?

Well, if you have ever tried to fast, you know it's not easy, and we don't like to suffer or feel inconvenienced, do we?

It's a relatively new discipline for me, one I am learning and growing in as I mature in my faith. I want to do more and be stronger, and while I wish I were superwoman and could say it's easy—it's not—at least for me. I imagine it's probably the same for most people. However, this doesn't mean that we can't continue to grow in it as a discipline.

The first time I experienced fasting was over fifteen years ago when a church we were attending challenged its members to commit to forty days of prayer and fasting. I chose to give up sugary drinks and did fine for the first thirty days until I developed a sinus headache. Experience had taught me that one of the fastest ways to get rid of one was to combine caffeinated soda with sinus medication. I struggled to know if I should give in and drink some to relieve my headache faster. Tony said, "God's not going to be mad at you because you have a soda to help make your headache go away."

So, I drank some.

And I didn't fast again for years until God had a good hold on me, and I knew He had asked me to pray for some pretty specific things. This time, I chose to abstain from eating from

9:00 a.m. until 5:00 p.m. and spent the afternoon praying and reading my Bible.

God met me there, and my energy was off the charts.

But my experience has not always been so easy. Three years ago, I decided to fast by giving up everything but water to drink and fruit and vegetables to eat. I love fruit and vegetables and didn't think it would be too hard.

The first day, I only felt a little dizzy, but it hit me harder on the second day after eating sautéed vegetables for breakfast. My stomach felt sick, and my head hurt. I didn't know what to do and prayed for God to guide me. I thought, *How can this be productive in any way?*

But during my prayer time, God spoke Psalm 84:5 to me: "Blessed are those whose strength is in you, whose hearts are set on pilgrimage." It's the same verse He has always given to me before we moved, and I prayed that if we were going to move again within the next year, that God would speak those words to Tony.

Two days later, He did, and five months after that, we said goodbye to our home of almost fourteen years.

You see, even in our weakness, God is faithful.

Part of my problem was that I hadn't eased into fasting by preparing my body to go without protein, dairy, sugar, fat, and caffeine. Now I understand how eliminating those things little by little is best so it will not shock my system. I am thankful that God is grace-filled, sees our desire to please Him, and meets us where we are.

My resolve was tested again when I was put on a liquid diet for almost forty-eight hours to prepare for a colonoscopy. I dreaded it so much because I had never gone for so long without solid food. But to my surprise, I found that I was not too hungry. People prayed for me, so I am certain that God's power sustained me, giving me extra energy. The experience proved that I could go without solid food for a time and be okay. God is still growing me and showing me new things.

Self-control is evidence of the Spirit's work in a believer's life according to 2 Timothy 1:7 (ESV) and Galatians 5:22–23 (ESV). In his letter to the Corinthians, the Apostle Paul wrote about how those who follow Christ must not allow fleshly desires to control them. "I will not be mastered by anything" (1 Corinthians 6:12). Because our bodies belong to Christ, everything we do must be for His glory. I may be weak in my power, but when I allow the Holy Spirit to work in and through me, His power enables me to do what I cannot do alone.

Don't stop trying to grow because you failed with a particular goal. Some people hate running. I ran cross country in high school and loved it. Running is about building strength and endurance and moving forward even when we want to stop. We get stronger with time, and I think the same thing happens with fasting.

There are many different ways to fast. Always check with your doctor if you choose to abstain from food or drink for a prolonged period. Some people have a difficult time because of medical conditions or require food or drink with their medications.

If food is not an option, you can fast from other things such as watching TV or using social media. Be creative. The goal is to spend more time with God and allow Him to pour into us, and there are many ways to do this.

Stand Together

During one of our many trips to Nashville to visit Taylor, we drove to one of our favorite places: Franklin, Tennessee. It's one of the nicest little towns that I have ever had the pleasure to visit. We loved the food at Merridee's Breadbasket and enjoyed exploring the lovely shops that lined the streets.

As we walked into Philanthropy, a clothing and more shop, I paused in front of a giant wooden prayer wall. Cards hung by hooks on the wall, and each one held a prayer request. Some were anonymous, while others included names. Customers could take a card and pray for that person or leave a prayer request.

As I stood there, an employee came and stood next to me. I told her how cool it was that they honor God in this way when so much of our culture tries to distance itself from Him. She said they could also pray with me.

At the time, I wanted to say yes. I would have loved to pray with her, but I was afraid she might do it right in the middle of the store. So, instead, I said, "Thank you."

Years ago, I was concerned with what others might think if they saw me pray in the middle of a boutique with a stranger. Since then, I have grown a little braver and think, if given the opportunity today, I would say yes.

If I ever make it to Franklin's Philanthropy store again, I hope to see the same lady and that she offers to pray with me. What a privilege. I love meeting people who live out their faith daily.

If you keep things to yourself rather than share them with others, I want to encourage you to begin to invite others to pray with you for the things that are on your heart. Be brave. Don't try to fight your battles alone. There is power in partnering with other believers and in praying for each other.

Jesus said, "If two of you on earth agree about anything they ask for, it will be done for them by my Father in heaven. For where two or three gather in my name, there am I with them" (Matthew 18:19-20).

We are stronger together.

When Joshua and the Israelites fought the Amalekites, "Moses, Aaron and Hur went to the top of the hill. As long as Moses held up his hands, the Israelites were winning, but whenever he lowered his hands, the Amalekites were winning" (Exodus 17:8–11). Can you imagine a battle around you while you stood, held your arms in the air, and could not drop them because your men would die?

We need each other, friend. When Moses became too tired, Aaron and Hur stood on either side of him and supported his hands until Joshua and the Israelites defeated the Amalekites (Exodus 17:12–13).

When we stand with others, we grow stronger and do better at the work God calls us to do.

How can you support someone today?

I have a team of people who are praying for me as I write this book. The enemy wages war against God's calling on me, and I cannot do it alone. Spiritual warfare is a real thing. However, "the one who is in [us] is greater than the one who is in the world" (1 John 4:4), so we fight, not with earthly weapons but with prayer, which can bring down "strongholds" (2 Corinthians 10:4).

When we speak His word, things happen.

For the word of God is alive and active.
                                                    Hebrews 4:12

My Grandma McAlexander was a woman of prayer. My mom said that she sat in her chair with her Bible, which contained photos of each of her grandchildren, and prayed for us. Grandma was an intercessor and often hosted Bible study groups in her home, so for those reasons, we always asked her to pray for us. It was part of her daily routine, not something she just did when she found the time.

I'm so thankful that she was a prayer warrior because I believe her prayers brought me to this space. Pray for your children, your grandchildren, and the ones not yet born.

Never stop praying.

You never know how God will use your prayers and what He may accomplish in others' lives because you chose to intercede and pray for them. We are stronger together.

Igniting Souls Conference

After signing on to publish my book with Author Academy Elite, Tony and I had the opportunity in 2018 to attend an event that was put on by my publisher, Kary Oberbrunner, the Igniting Souls Conference.[1] In the days leading up to the conference, I wrote out a prayer list in my journal, asking God to help me to be brave and willing to step outside of my comfort zone.

I asked for Him to arrange divine connections, place me at tables with people He wanted me to meet, help me to hear His voice, and guide me in the way to go.

During the four-day conference, God's plans unfolded. As we walked into the hotel restaurant for breakfast, three other ladies walked in behind us. As the host approached to ask us how many, I said, "Two," and then turned to the three ladies behind me and said, "Unless you would like to join us." They agreed, so the five of us sat down at a table together.

I had a pre-session prayer meeting before our day started, so Tony and I went through the buffet line and sat down to eat. The other women at the table were from Israel, the United Kingdom, and North Carolina. They asked me about my book. As I shared my thoughts and concerns, they encouraged me to follow God's lead.

The conversation was full of affirmation, and as I excused myself to go to the pre-session prayer meeting, I knew God had answered my prayers. A couple of days later, one of the ladies approached me in our large meeting room and asked if I would join her and four other ladies for a mastermind group to share ideas, resources, and encouragement.

God also put two people I had prayed to meet at our table. I had heard Dan (New York Times best-selling author of *48 Days to the Work You Love*) and Joanne Miller (author of *Creating a Haven of Peace*) speak on Niccie Kliegl's show "Living Within the Sweet Spot."[2] Their words were inspirational for me, so I asked God (and recorded it in my journal) to allow me the opportunity to meet both of them. I could hardly believe it when they were speakers for our conference and sat at our table.

While I was gone, Tony had a conversation with Dan. He said they talked about Franklin and Merridee's and about me writing a book.

When I returned to the table, Dan graciously asked me about my book. In a room filled with hundreds of people, God blessed me with the opportunity to meet this inspiring person.

Friend, God is so good. Nothing is too hard for Him.

So, we wait in hopeful anticipation of what lies ahead.

What has He laid on your heart to pray for?

Are you praying bold prayers that only God can answer, or are you settling for less because you don't understand His incredible power and love for you? He is a good Father who gives good gifts to His children.

> *Every good and perfect gift is from above, coming down from the Father of the heavenly lights, who does not change like shifting shadows.*
>
> James 1:17

> *If you, then, though you are evil, know how to give good gifts to your children, how much more will your Father in heaven give good gifts to those who ask him!*
>
> Matthew 7:11

I prayed so long for God to give me mentors, people who were doing what I knew He had called me to do. The Igniting Souls Tribe provided me with a network of like-minded, faith-filled people to learn from and walk alongside as we dreamed and created things together.

PRAYING BOLD PRAYERS

Trusting God When It's Hard

Dreaming and planning for the future is a natural part of life. Without a strategy, we have no direction. But what happens when you find that God's plans for you look vastly different from the ones you created for yourself?

From the moment my sister, Karen, and her husband, Doug, were married, they knew they wanted to have children. Karen became pregnant the first year and was overjoyed to become a mother. But before she and Doug could even begin preparations to welcome their child into the world, Karen suffered a miscarriage. They were devastated and hoped and prayed, but Karen did not get pregnant again during the next five years.

She wondered if her dream was possible. "I grieved not being able to conceive and give birth," she said. "Every other person I knew was getting pregnant and having babies except me."

An acquaintance familiar with their troubles put them in touch with the son of a missionary couple who ran a children's home in Guatemala. Karen was unsure, as she had never considered adopting an older child. But when they saw the picture of nine-year-old Juan, they knew he was the child God had selected for them. Nine months later, they traveled to Guatemala City, and Juan came back to the United States with two parents who were ready to love him to pieces.

Karen and Doug felt in awe of how God had blessed them and Juan. "We are so thankful God put us together. He is such a good kid and such a blessing." However, with still more love to give, Karen's heart *ached for a baby*. Again, God found a way to answer her prayers.

While at a conference, they ran into a friend and fellow pastor. He shocked Karen when, out of the blue, he turned to her and said, "You need a baby, don't you?" He gave Karen and Doug the number of an attorney who worked with a crisis pregnancy center and knew an expectant mother who wanted to place her baby for adoption. Karen and Doug wrote a letter to the woman, poured out their hopes on paper, and prayed that she would see their desire to love and care for this child. The woman chose them, and soon, they came home with son number two. They named him Jadin, which means "God has heard."

Four years and many prayers later, Karen and Doug adopted their third son, Hunter. For five years, my sister and brother-and-law had tried and failed to conceive, but God blessed them with three sons and a household full of love.

Karen felt fully emboldened by how God had blessed her with His answered prayers. Despite being unable to get pregnant for years, she and Doug decided that it was the right time to take more ambitious measures.

Karen suffered from endometriosis, a condition in which the uterine tissue begins to develop on surrounding organs. She also had a lot of scar tissue built up from previous surgeries.

As suggested by her doctor, she agreed to be part of an experimental study in which she underwent two surgeries. The first (a laparoscopy) removed the endometriosis and scar tissue, followed by pumping a trial solution into her abdomen, hoping it would reduce the scar tissue typically left behind due to the scraping during the laparoscopy. The second surgery would determine if the solution worked by reducing the amount of scar tissue post-surgery.

Before the second surgery, Karen asked the elders of her church to anoint her with oil and pray for God to open up her womb and make it fertile and for the endometriosis to be completely gone.

She said she wanted the surgeon to be "flabbergasted by what he found."

After the surgeries, the doctor couldn't believe what he saw. He told Doug, "I'm flabbergasted!" *Yes, he used that exact word.* "Karen's abdomen looks brand new." The surgeries worked far better than anyone had expected.

Not long after, Karen became pregnant for the first time in eleven years. Sadly, this pregnancy also ended in miscarriage. She became pregnant, once more, four months later but was again unable to carry the pregnancy to term. Though shaken by the loss of two more pregnancies, Karen and Doug still saw the hand of God at work. For over a decade, they were unable to *get* pregnant. But after anointing with oil and praying with their church elders, they had managed to get pregnant twice within months.

A decade later, Karen found out that researchers did not believe that the trial solution pumped into her abdomen after her laparoscopy benefitted the patients who participated in the study.

This piece of information strengthened Karen's belief that the breakthrough she experienced was because of God's intervention and not a result of the procedure itself.

Karen now believes that there is a reason God didn't allow either pregnancy to last. "In all reality, He may have saved me from something unknown, but I won't know this side of heaven."

With time, peace settled over Karen and Doug. Their desire to bear a child subsided, and with increasing wisdom and grace, they continued to rejoice in the three gifts God had given them. "We would never choose a different path from the one we traveled because it led us to our children," she adds. "We couldn't imagine life without them."

Four years ago, Karen faced testing again when she was diagnosed with ovarian cancer, following a hysterectomy. She was "scared out of her mind," terrified at the thought of leaving Doug and their three sons behind. But she was also wiser, more faithful than ever, and fully knew the potential of God's healing powers.

Karen called on her church's elders to anoint her with oil and pray over her. They prayed that the biopsies would show no cancer in surrounding areas and that it had not metastasized. Results showed only a tiny spot of cancer in tissue outside the ovary, so the oncologist ordered six rounds of chemotherapy to take care of any unseen cancer cells in her body. Chemotherapy is a grueling process that takes a severe toll on the body, but Karen had God and an army of friends, family, and even strangers to pray for her and give her strength.

God's word is called the "sword of the Spirit," and a sword is a weapon in battle, part of the spiritual armor Paul talks about in Ephesians.[3] Jesus used God's word to defeat Satan when He was in the wilderness, so we followed His example.[4] Karen and our mom chose the following scriptures, and we prayed those scriptures as prayers back to God on her behalf:

Delight yourself in the LORD, and he will give you the desires of your heart.

Psalm 37:4 ESV

Our prayer: "We delight in you, Lord, and you promise to give us the desires of our hearts. Our desire is for Karen to be free of cancer and for there to be no recurrence."

You will keep in perfect peace those whose minds are steadfast, because they trust in you.

Isaiah 26:3

Our prayer: "Karen is trusting in you, Lord, and we trust that you will keep her in perfect peace."

Hear me and answer me. My thoughts trouble me and I am distraught.

Psalm 55:2

Our prayer: "Lord, we pray that when Karen feels distraught and thoughts trouble her, you will hear her prayers and answer her with your peace."

> *Praise the LORD, my soul; all my inmost being, praise his holy name. Praise the LORD, my soul, and forget not all his benefits—who forgives all your sins and heals all your diseases, who redeems your life from the pit and crowns you with love and compassion.*
>
> Psalm 103:1–4

Our prayer: Karen personalized and prayed this verse.

> *Praise the LORD. . . who forgives all [my] sins and heals all [my]diseases, who redeems [my] life from the pit and crowns [me]with love and compassion.*

One sweet little girl had prayed for Karen, and when her mother reminded her to do so again, she responded, "She's already healed, Mama. Jesus healed her."

At the end of her chemotherapy, there was no cancer in Karen's body. She says, "Fear still takes hold with every little ache and pain. I try to pray through it and not let the fear linger and pray for my desires but also try to pray 'thy will be done.' Thinking about the possibility of not having much time left on this earth has given me an urgency to share the gospel with those God puts on my heart. I believe God has a bigger plan for me and needed to allow this cancer to steer me in a different direction. It certainly has slowed me down and has given me more time to draw closer to Him."

Surrender comes to mind when I think of my sister and her bravery. Bravery doesn't mean that we are unafraid. It means that we choose to trust God and turn our burdens over to Him. Pray boldly to find your bravery. Turn to each other and turn to God. Even when we are gripped by fear, God is there, and He is listening. May we all be like Karen and say, "Thy will be done."

Align yourself with God and pray bold prayers. Our God is amazing. Why would we ever not trust Him?

What bold prayers do you need to pray? What is stopping you?

Chapter 14
ARE YOU READY?

My Grandma McAlexander lived her life ready to meet Jesus, which is also my desire. I want to fulfill His plans for me while I am on this earth and not leave anything undone.

During her final moments in the hospital with congestive heart failure, my Uncle Kal was with her. I asked him to share the story with me so I could share it with you.

Dear Kristi,

I did spend the night with your grandma after the doctor told us she wouldn't last through it. About 2:00 a.m., she roused and began to call, "Elroy, over here. Elroy, over here," waving her arm in an inviting motion. I took her hand and asked, "Is Dad coming to get you, Mom?" She settled down and fell back to sleep.

About 4:00 a.m., she roused again and began to call out, "Jesus, over here. Jesus, over here," waving her arm in the same way. Again, I took her hand and asked, "Are Dad and Jesus coming to get you, Mom?" She settled down and fell back to sleep.

About 6:00 a.m., she roused a third time. Her breathing was very heavy. At first, I couldn't make out what she was trying to say. She would take a breath and get out "Hur..." and then another breath and get out "...ry." After a few times of repeating those two syllables, it dawned on me that she was saying, "Hurry." So, I asked, "Mom, are Dad and Jesus coming to get you? Are you in a hurry to go? It's okay to go. Go be with Dad and Jesus." She quieted and breathed her last breath.

The rest of the story took place at the funeral where I shared the story of her passing. After the service, the group of younger ladies Mom had studied and prayed with for twenty plus years approached me. One said, "Kal, we have another explanation for what you heard. We have been praying with your mom for over twenty years. She was NOT afraid to tell Jesus what to do. We don't think she was saying she was in a hurry. She was telling Jesus and Elroy to hurry because she thought they were moving too slowly."

Either way, your grandma was not only unafraid to enter into the presence of her Lord, Savior, and Friend, Jesus Christ, she was anxious to. She was at the very least in a HURRY to.

Wow! This story gives me goosebumps. I want to live my life in such a way that I know without a doubt that I am ready to meet Him when He returns.

We all have an expiration date.

Are you ready to meet Jesus? Do you know Him as your Lord and Savior?

All our accumulated wealth and things of this earth cannot help us as we slip from this life into the next. What is waiting on the other side for you?

Jesus said, "I am the way and the truth and the life. No one comes to the Father except through me" (John 14:6).

Friend, the Bible tells us that Jesus is the only way to God, and while you still have breath in your lungs, you have the opportunity to make things right with Him. Don't wait until it's too late.

We all have a finite number of days on this earth. Most of us don't know our number, but God knows. What we do with our life on this earth matters for eternity.

The Bible tells us that "all have sinned and fall short of the glory of God" (Romans 3:23) and that our sin separates us from God who is holy (Isaiah 59:2). For this reason, He sent Jesus to earth to die on the cross. Jesus became the final sacrifice, took our sins upon Himself, and through His shed blood, cleaned us before God (Acts 10:34–43; Hebrews 10:10). We are righteous in His eyes.[1]

When God looks at us, He sees us through His son. Isn't that beautiful?

We have assurance that "if we confess our sins, he is faithful and just and will forgive us our sins and purify us from all unrighteousness" (1 John 1:9).

It doesn't matter how you have messed up. God forgives and offers eternal life with Him. What a gift.

When Peter preached on the Day of Pentecost, the people were "cut to the heart" and asked, "What shall we do?" "Peter replied, 'Repent and be baptized, every one of you, in the name of Jesus Christ for the forgiveness of your sins. And you will receive the gift of the Holy Spirit'" (Acts 2:37–38).

Genuine repentance is more than saying, "I'm sorry. Forgive me." It's also the desire to live differently and the subsequent action that turns one away from sin and back toward God.

God knows every thought, every word we speak, and every action we take. He knows our hearts, and He knows if we are truly trying to live for Him or not.

While in our earthly bodies, we will never be perfect and without sin. But the beauty of repentance and forgiveness is that God's grace covers us. He wants to see us grow more like Jesus every day.

Without the power of the Holy Spirit, this would not be possible.

Life in the Spirit is amazing and challenging. It often invites us to step outside of our comfort zone and encourages us to move forward in all that God calls us to do, even if we feel afraid. It means we *go* even when we cannot see the whole road ahead. And *maybe* we even get a little braver because we get to see how God takes care of us.

As we get to know Him better, we see He is trustworthy.

Jesus' disciples knew there was a cost to follow Him (Luke 14:25–33). They saw everything firsthand and understood that what they would receive was greater than anything they would lose.

Jesus told them, "My Father's house has many rooms; if that were not so, would I have told you that I am going there to prepare a place for you? And if I go and prepare a place for you, I will come back and take you to be with me that you also may be where I am" (John 14:2–3).

Paul was joyful and even boasted about the adversity he suffered (Romans 5:3–5 NLT; 2 Corinthians 11:16–33 NLT). Why would anyone do that unless they were certain of what was on the other side of this life?

God moves mountains (Mark 11:22–24). He owns "the cattle on a thousand hills" (Psalm 50:10) and has access to anything and everything we could ever need. He mends and softens hearts (Ezekiel 36:26–27)—the ultimate relationship healer. He opens prison doors and sets people free, literally (Acts 12:5–11) and figuratively (Galatians 5).

Nothing is impossible for Him. Sickness and disease? God has the power to heal. Addiction? He can help you find freedom. Fear and anxiety? He can help you overcome any obstacle.

And the coolest thing ever is that He wants you to come to Him as you are.

Don't wait until you feel *good enough*, which is what the enemy wants. He knows if you allow God into your life, God's power can change you, so He makes you think you have to *fix* yourself before God accepts you.

The enemy lies.

The truth is that if you come to Him, God will help you do what you cannot do on your own. The God who raised Jesus from the dead can handle anything, and the most wonderful thing about being His son or daughter is that the same God who does all of these things lives in us in the form of His Holy Spirit. If you are a child of God, His power is alive in you. Nothing is impossible with God.

He cannot fail.

We know that we are on the winning team when we are on God's side, trying to live in obedience. Let's put on our shoes of faith and stay in the "race" until He calls us home.[2]

I want to stand before Him one day, knowing I left it all on the field—that I didn't hold anything back but fulfilled my purpose on earth. I want to hear Him say, "Well done, good and faithful servant" (Matthew 25:23)!

It's not possible in my power alone, so I'm thankful to know that His power is at work in and around me.

I may be an ordinary girl, but my God is extraordinary, and life with Him is amazing because I know I am never alone and I have a secure future. I have someone who is always fighting for me. Because of that, I can live an extraordinary life. And so can you.

If you are a child of God, you have a secure future in Him.

Are you ready to meet Jesus? Why or why not?
What do you need to do to be ready?

Chapter 15
ADVENTURE INVOLVES RISK

Over the years, Tony has lovingly encouraged me to step outside of my comfort zone. In doing so, I have flown in a private plane, ridden a Segway over the rough terrain of the Sonoran Desert, and eaten the fruit from the inside of a teddy bear cholla cactus. I have watched a blue whale and her baby swim next to our boat, twelve miles out in the Pacific Ocean, and braved the rough, salty waves of the Pacific during a surfing lesson. God also had another adventure in mind.

I couldn't sleep one night in early June 2017. I looked up at the ceiling, prayed, and listened for God's voice. The word *fearless* flashed into my mind, so I prayed that I would be fearless with God's plans for me. I also prayed for a loved one who was facing a difficult situation and prayed for God to make Tony's workload more manageable while he was covering for a colleague who had left the company. I heard the words *realign* and *reassign* in my spirit and believed that God told me to pray those two words on behalf of Tony and his job.

For fourteen months, I continued to pray this specific way, and then one night, I had a dream we were moving again. I looked to my right and saw a glass door. I could not access the door through conventional means, so I found a middle section to raise and knew I would have to access the door unconventionally.

I wrote the dream down in my journal but kept it to myself for the time being. It was late summer 2018, and as Tony and I drove to the Kansas State Fair two weeks later, I told him about my dream.

He found it interesting because a week earlier, a colleague said Tony's name was mentioned for a position, which could once again move us back to the city. Interestingly enough, it was a different path from the one we had always thought would be the case. Within a couple of weeks, two more co-workers nonchalantly mentioned the same information to Tony. Although we didn't yet have any solid confirmation or a time frame, we knew something was happening.

A few months later, Tony learned that changes were coming. He was encouraged to apply for this specific position when the time came, and he did.

In 2019, we moved from comfortable Manhattan, Kansas back to the city. This time, our kids did not follow. They were all adults, so our moves and theirs didn't have to sync. I felt excited for every opportunity the city held, but I missed our kids and our only granddaughter (at that time)—*a lot*. It brought me comfort to know we were within God's will, so I chose to look at it as another adventure.

About a month after our move, I attended a conference at a large church in California. As I sat in the auditorium, a young woman named Valeria scooted over to introduce herself. I had registered for the conference months in advance, so my nametag said I was from Kansas. She acknowledged that I had crossed out Kansas and written Iowa on my nametag, so I explained to her how we had moved.

She paused for a moment and said, "I'm getting 'promotion.'"

I said, "Yes, my husband received a promotion. That's why we moved."

ADVENTURE INVOLVES RISK

She said, "No, I think it's promotion for you. I believe you will be planting seeds, and you will need to take some risks."

I believe God spoke those words through her. There were hundreds of people there. What were the odds that I would sit a few feet away from this young woman and out of the blue, she would give me this message?

God knows where you are. He sees you and knows the plans He has for your life.

He calls us to **R.I.S.K.** everything for Him.

Run Your Race: God has designed a life for us.

> *I have fought the good fight, I have finished the race, I have kept the faith. Now there is in store for me the crown of righteousness, which the Lord, the righteous Judge, will award to me on that day—and not only to me, but also to all who have longed for his appearing.*
>
> 2 Timothy 4:7–8

Instruction: We need to receive our instructions from God.

> *If any of you lacks wisdom, you should ask God, who gives generously to all without finding fault, and it will be given to you. But when you ask, you must believe and not doubt, because the one who doubts is like a wave of the sea, blown and tossed by the wind. That person should not expect to receive anything from the Lord.*
>
> James 1:5–7

Surrender: We have to decide in our hearts to trust Him and be obedient to what He calls us to do.

> *Consequently, faith comes from hearing the message, and the message is heard through the word about Christ.*
>
> Romans 10:17

Knock: We have to take action. We have to step out in faith and open the door.

> *Ask and it will be given to you; seek and you will find; knock and the door will be opened to you. For everyone who asks receives; the one who seeks finds; and to the one who knocks, the door will be opened.*
> *Matthew 7:7–8*

> *Here I am! I stand at the door and knock. If anyone hears my voice and opens the door, I will come in and eat with that person, and they with me.*
> *Revelation 3:20*

> *"But my righteous one will live by faith. And I take no pleasure in the one who shrinks back." But we do not belong to those who shrink back and are destroyed, but to those who have faith and are saved.*
> *Hebrews 10:38–39*

By the way, Valeri[a] means "brave" or "courageous."[1] I want to be brave. Though I still have moments of fear, it's okay. What's important is that I don't allow it to control me. I have not come this far with God to stop now, and I have committed in my heart to step into everything He has for me. At times, I am terrified and at other times, I am exhilarated by all of it. If faith without "good deeds...is dead and useless" (James 2:17 NLT), we have to step into the opportunities that God puts before us if we want to live an extraordinary life.

Adventure usually contains an element of risk because there is something unknown. I don't always like that, but God calls us to be brave.

What if living only for what *feels* secure is not really living at all? What if God has some amazing things in store for us if we just trusted Him enough to say yes?

ADVENTURE INVOLVES RISK

Tony and I have spent the last two years finding our footing in our new city—just the two of us—for the first time in many years. We are now serving in a new church and trusting God to help us find our place within our new community.

I know God has a plan because *He always does*. And I know it is good because God is good.

As I finish this book, I am praying about the next things He has in mind for me—for us. I hope to have conversations with people to encourage them. I hope to help others put fear in its proper place and take hold of everything God has planned for their lives. I want to leave a legacy of faith for our children and grandchildren.

I look forward to more adventures with Tony. When we celebrated our wedding anniversary, one of our purchases was a bucket list book for couples. I want to make the most of each and every day with my best friend.

Being brave looks different for all of us. But one thing I know is that the life you were designed to have is on the other side of surrender. It's not always an easy journey, but I can promise you it is worth it.

You cannot fulfill God's plans for your life alone. But in the arms of our loving and mighty God and backed by the power of the Holy Spirit, you *can* live an extraordinary life. You were created for it. Are you ready to begin the adventure?

God calls you to be brave and live the adventure He has planned for you.

What does bravery look like for you?
What are you willing to risk for God?

ABOUT THE AUTHOR

Former stay-at-home mom, turned graduate student, turned author and speaker, Kristine Kimmi understands what it's like to love her roles as a wife and mom to the best people in the world and still long for the opportunity to use the talents and gifts God wove into her DNA for His glory. Through her God-led journey, she has discovered that when we put fear in its proper place and move forward with God's plans, our ordinary lives are transformed into extraordinary lives of adventure. Kristine and her husband, Tony, have three daughters, one son-in-law, two granddaughters, and reside in Iowa.

WHAT WILL YOU R.I.S.K.?

ARE YOU READY TO EXPLORE YOUR NEXT ADVENTURE WITH GOD?

Visit
KristineKimmi.com

NOTES

Chapter 2

1. Kristine Kimmi, "Invitation to a Life-Changing Experience with Prayer," August 21, 2017, https://www.kristinekimmi.com/blog/invitation-to-a-life-changing-experience-with-prayer.

2. Becky Tirabassi, *Let Prayer Change Your Life: Discover the Awesome Power of, Empowering Discipline of, and Ultimate Design for Prayer* (Nashville, TN: Thomas Nelson, Copyright ©1992 by Becky Tirabassi), back cover. Used by permission of Thomas Nelson. www.thomasnelson.com.

3. Charles R. Swindoll, *Joseph: A Man of Integrity and Forgiveness* (Nashville, TN: Word Publishing, Copyright ©1998 by Charles R. Swindoll, Inc.), 116. Used by permission of Thomas Nelson. www.thomasnelson.com.

4. See Lamentations 3:37.

5. 1 Peter 4:10; Hebrews 13:20–21.

Chapter 4

1. Kristine Kimmi, "How to Respond When God Turns Your World Upside Down," December 23, 2016, https://www.kristinekimmi.com/blog/how-to-respond-when-god-turns-your-world-upside-down. Quote appeared in a blog post titled "Seasons of Change," originally published October 24, 2012.

2. Mark 11:22–24.

Chapter 5

1. Ezekiel 36:8.

2. Luke 1:37 ESV.

Chapter 7

1. Jennie Allen, *Anything: The Prayer That Unlocked My God and My Soul* (Nashville, TN: W Publishing Group, Copyright © 2011 by Jennie Allen).

2. Jennie Allen, *Nothing to Prove: Why We Can Stop Trying So Hard* (Colorado Springs, CO: WaterBrook, Copyright © 2017 by Jennie Allen).

3. Lamentations 3:37; Job 1.

Chapter 8

1. 2 Timothy 3:16.

2. See Acts 10:19–20.

NOTES

3. In the Bible, we see God's messages being delivered through His prophets. Believers are to exhort and encourage each other and share the gospel with unbelievers (1 Timothy 4:13; 2 Timothy 4:2; 1 Thessalonians 4:18; Hebrews 10:25; Matthew 28:19-20).

4. Psalm 19:1-4; Romans 1:20.

5. See Genesis 37:5-11; Matthew 1:20-25, 2:12.

6. See Isaiah 6; Acts 10:3-16.

7. See 1 Samuel 3:4-21.

8. See Luke 1:26-38, 2:8-15; Hebrews 13:2.

9. Sagan Hundley, "At the End of Myself," *His Redeeming Pursuit*, August 22, 2016. https://hisredeemingpursuit.com/2016/08/22/at-the-end-of-myself/. Used by permission.

10. Oswald Chambers, "I Indeed…But He" in *My Utmost for His Highest: An Updated Edition in Today's Language*, ed. James Reimann (Grand Rapids, MI: Discovery House Publishers, Copyright © 1992 by Oswald Chambers Publications Association, Ltd.), August 22. All rights reserved. Used by permission of Discovery House Publishers.

11. John 15:5 NKJV.

12. Adam F. Thompson and Adrian Beale, *The Divinity Code to Understanding Your Dreams and Visions* (Shippensburg, PA: Destiny Image Publishers, Copyright © 2011 Adam F. Thompson and Adrian Beale), 385. All rights reserved. Used by permission of Destiny Image Publishers.

13. Thompson and Beale, *The Divinity Code*, 226.

14. Thompson and Beale, *The Divinity Code*, 522-23.

15. Thompson and Beale, *The Divinity Code*, 486. Also see Ephesians 6:15, ESV and Colossians 1:15–23.

16. John 14:27, 16:33; Romans 5:1–11.

17. Thompson and Beale, *The Divinity Code*, 589.

18. Thompson and Beale, *The Divinity Code*, 523. Also see Ephesians 3:16.

19. Thompson and Beale, *The Divinity Code*, 392–93.

20. Sandie Freed, *Understanding Your Dreams: How to Unlock the Meaning of God's Messages* (Bloomington, MN: Chosen Books, Copyright © 2017 by Sandie Freed), 130.

21. See 1 Kings 3:4–15; Matthew 1:20–25.

22. See Daniel 4.

23. Two books that I have in my library are *The Divinity Code to Understanding Your Dreams and Visions* by Adam F. Thompson and Adrian Beale and *Understanding Your Dreams: How to Unlock the Meaning of God's Messages* by Sandie Freed.

24. Daniel 2:28.

25. Isaiah 55:9.

Chapter 9

1. Adam F. Thompson and Adrian Beale, *The Divinity Code to Understanding Your Dreams and Visions* (Shippensburg, PA: Destiny Image Publishers, Copyright © 2011 Adam F. Thompson and Adrian Beale), 549. All rights reserved. Used by permission of Destiny Image Publishers.

NOTES

2. Anne Graham Lotz, "Be Ready to Meet Jesus," Facebook photo, January 29, 2017. https://www.facebook.com/149929282475/photos/a.10151085215612476/10154422327402476.

3. Jennie Allen, *Anything: The Prayer That Unlocked My God and My Soul* (Nashville, TN: W Publishing Group, Copyright © 2011 by Jennie Allen), xiv. Used by permission of Thomas Nelson. www.thomasnelson.com.

4. Thompson and Beale, *The Divinity Code*, 317, 395, 508–09. Also see 1 Corinthians 16:9 and Genesis 3:1–15.

5. See Isaiah 57:14.

Chapter 10

1. Adam F. Thompson and Adrian Beale, *The Divinity Code to Understanding Your Dreams and Visions* (Shippensburg, PA: Destiny Image Publishers, Copyright © 2011 Adam F. Thompson and Adrian Beale), 266. All rights reserved. Used by permission of Destiny Image Publishers.

2. 2 Kings 6:17.

3. 2 Kings 6:18-22.

4. 2 Kings 6:23.

Chapter 11

1. Isaiah 52:1, emphasis added.

2. Isaiah 52:2, emphasis added.

Chapter 12

1. Kristine Kimmi, "Regaining Peace of Mind When Faced with Anxiety and Fear," March 4, 2017. https://kristinekimmi.com/blog/regaining-peace-of-mind-when-faced-with-anxiety-and-fear.
2. Numbers 13:28.
3. Numbers 13:30.
4. Numbers 14:10.
5. Numbers 14:37.
6. Numbers 14:40–43.
7. Acts 8:26–31.
8. Acts 8:31–35.
9. Acts 8:36–39.

Chapter 13

1. Author Academy Elite (https://authoracademyelite.com); Igniting Souls Conference (https://ignitingsoulsconference.com).
2. Niccie Kliegl, Living Within the Sweet Spot, podcast, iTunes May 29, 2018, "Wise Choices Work, 'The Problem' What Motivates Your Decisions?"
3. Ephesians 6:10–20.
4. Matthew 4:1–11; Deuteronomy 6:13,16; Deuteronomy 8:3.

NOTES

Chapter 14

1. 2 Corinthians 5:21.
2. 2 Timothy 4:7–8.

Chapter 15

1. Adam F. Thompson and Adrian Beale, *The Divinity Code to Understanding Your Dreams and Visions* (Shippensburg, PA: Destiny Image Publishers, Copyright © 2011 Adam F. Thompson and Adrian Beale), 650. All rights reserved. Used by permission of Destiny Image Publishers.

CPSIA information can be obtained
at www.ICGtesting.com
Printed in the USA
BVHW011810100622
639499BV00002B/38